food for
cooks

Clare Ferguson

photography by David Munns

food for
cooks

jacqui
small

To all food lovers
who know there will always be
more to discover
and to all those dear to me
for their forbearance

First published in 2003 by Jacqui Small,
an imprint of Aurum Press Ltd, 25 Bedford Avenue,
London WC1B 3AT

Publisher Jacqui Small
Art Director Janet James
Food Stylist Clare Ferguson
Props Stylist Victoria Allen
Project Editor Emily Hatchwell
Recipe Editor Madeline Weston
Production Geoff Barlow

British Library Cataloguing-in-Publication Data
A catalogue record for this book is available
from the British Library

ISBN: 1 903221 17 X

Printed and bound in China

RECIPE NOTES

Spoon measurements Recipes use standard measuring
spoons (5ml for teaspoon, 15ml for tablespoon).
Spoon measurements are level unless otherwise stated.
Ovens Recipes in this book were tested with a fan-
assisted oven. If using a conventional oven, increase the
temperature by 20°C, or follow the manufacturer's
instructions.
Microwave ovens Where a microwave oven was used,
this was at 750–900 watts on High or Full; if using a
microwave oven that is appreciably lower or higher in
wattage, timings should be adjusted accordingly.
Herbs Fresh herbs are used unless otherwise stated.
If substituting dried herbs, use a half or a quarter of the
amount, or substitute another fresh herb.
Oils Use the oils specified whenever possible, and avoid
any vegetable oils of unidentifiable provenance.
Butter If neither salted or unsalted butter is specified,
use your own preferred kind.
Eggs are large, unless specified otherwise.
Raw foods Dishes containing raw or partly cooked eggs,
raw milk cheeses, raw or rare-cooked meat or fish
products should not be served to very young children
or to the elderly, or to anyone who is pregnant.
Serving temperature For reasons of safety, foods that are
served hot or warm should be eaten within 90 minutes;
if more time elapses, they should be refrigerated.

contents

introduction

Good cooking is not about luxury ingredients, it is about everyday resourcefulness, creativity and inspiration. Curiosity helps, as does a sense of humour about the mysteries of the kitchen.

These pages and pictures are for all those cooks who long to discover more about food and cooking but don't know where to start; and for all food lovers who like vivid, interesting flavours, or who enjoy exotic or deeply traditional foods but need help in turning them into a delicious dish.

Producing real, simple meals from scratch, day by day, using decent raw materials, is an underrated skill. It sometimes seems harder to achieve as our free time shrinks and as 'ready meals' beckon from the supermarket display cabinets. Available time for food shopping, once one of life's more enjoyable leisure pursuits, often loses out to DIY, overdue housework or dealing with the email inbox.

True hospitality is an instinct, but spur-of-the-moment invitations to lunch or dinner may often depend on a well-stocked pantry.

What are foods for cooks?

The more than 500 ingredients chosen for inclusion in this book – some basic, some esoteric – are a personal selection. What these storecupboard foods, drinks, flavourings and cooking aids have in common is that they have all been preserved or packaged in some way, so they can be bought in advance and stored on a shelf for days, weeks or even months.

Once upon a time, preserved foods consisted of a small range of worthy ingredients put away for emergencies or the winter. Today, however, our storecupboards and pantries are crammed with a vast range of intriguing and versatile preserved foods from all corners of the country and the world. Interestingly, in this modern era of refrigeration and globally accessible fresh foods, we eat preserved foods not so much out of necessity but simply because we enjoy the taste.

This book evaluates the potential of all these ingredients and provides hundreds of ideas for using them – combined or not with the fresh foods that we must buy on a more regular basis. Of course, it is unthinkable to live without fresh milk, bread, eggs, herbs and garlic, not to mention fresh fruit and vegetables and fresh meat and fish, but good larder ingredients will give fluency, freedom and fascination to your cooking and will also help you to produce stylish and relaxed meals. They are the secret weapon that can transform reasonable raw materials into inspirational dishes and help make cooking fun.

Authenticity of ingredients

Decent cooking is knowing how to use "common ingredients produced uncommonly well", to quote the superb Irish cook, Myrtle Allen. It is also knowing how to select the right ones for the task. The best long-life foods are those whose tastes, textures and appearances have not been compromised. Some modifications are delicious, others are not.

An important clue as to the quality of any food, from biscuit to bacon, is that, generally, you get what you pay for. You can also judge from a short, honest ingredients list – which should include few or no additives such as stabilisers, colourants, flavourings or preservatives – whether the food is a properly prepared food or an industrial product made out of the left-overs of another manufacturing process, or simply a low-quality product.

Understanding the label

The ingredients list states, on Tabasco sauce, for example, simply 'vinegar, red pepper and salt'; on chocolate paste, 'chocolate, sugar syrup, cream'. (Ingredients are listed in order of the volume used.) Many foods, however, contain more complex ingredients than this, including E numbers. Despite their bad press, not all E numbers are to be shunned. They are merely a form of classification for additives such as colourings, flavourants, preservatives and stabilisers. Some of these are certainly not a welcome addition to food, but others are perfectly acceptable. Glucose syrup, vitamin C and tartaric acid – cooking aids included in this book – all have E numbers.

'Nature identical' flavours (that is, chemically identical to the natural flavour) are laboratory-created but can enhance some foods if used wisely, although natural flavours are, of course, the ideal. Truffle oil, for example, may be flavoured with both real truffle fragments and nature identical flavourings.

Another clue as to the quality of any product is whether it has a 'denomination' – the defined, strictly regulated identity, based on geographical location, that distinguishes a particular (often artisanal) product from any other like it. Terms used to denote this, such as AOC (Appellation d'Origine Contrôlée) in France, and DOC (Denominazione di Origine Controllata) in Italy, can apply to cheese, butter, vinegar and even lentils, as well as, most famously, to wines. (There is no equivalent in Britain.) If you buy Parmesan cheese that doesn't proudly state its denomination, you are not buying a product of guaranteed quality. Someone once quipped "Never buy anything not signed", and it is not a bad maxim.

The important issues of organic or sustainable production, along with genetic modification, must be matters for personal debate: so choose for yourself.

The preservation process

Preservation, whether of artisanal or of mass-market foods, can be achieved by drying, pickling, salting, curing, smoking or heating – that is, by changing the normal concentration of liquid within the food's cells. Air, sun, heat, acids, sugars, syrups, fats, spices, herbs, waxes and alcohols can all be used to lengthen a food's shelf life. So can appropriate packaging.

Thanks to modern technological advancements, methods to prolong the 'keepability' of foods have been revolutionised over recent decades. Foods may now come gas-packed, vacuum-packed, pasteurised, ultra-heat-treated, sterilised, semi-cooked ('mi-cuit'), kiln-dried or freeze-dried. And pop-top, pull-tab and other inventive seals now offer tamper-proof ways to close containers and ensure freshness and safety. Not all such methods produce good results all of the time, however. You must experiment, taste and decide for yourself which foods you like.

Even when buying products with a famously long shelf life, such as pulses or grains, it is generally best to buy foods little and often. Even if lentils and rice are perfectly usable after one year, their flavour will certainly have deteriorated.

The fridge is an undeniably useful storage place, but many foods taste better if stored in a cool, dark but not refrigerated place, whether it is a walk-in pantry or a cupboard. Perishable foods should be kept in the fridge in the hottest months of the year, but most cheeses, for example, have a much better flavour if kept out of the fridge.

How to buy the best

There are many ways to access the global larder and enjoy the world's best ingredients. Get to know and appreciate the street markets, farmers' markets and farm shops, if they exist, in your area. Make an effort to explore every kind of food shop, including ethnic grocers, specialist delicatessens, wholefood shops and luxury department stores. Wherever immigrant communities thrive, you will find a rich source of interesting and unusual foodstuffs, and their shops allow you to learn about their food culture at first hand. In recent decades, supermarkets have massively changed our consumer purchasing habits, in some ways for the worse, but they have, at the same time, brought international foods to a wider audience.

Mail-order suppliers, often with the help of the Internet, have also tapped into what modern, time-poor shoppers need: individual service and good ingredients.

This book

Food for Cooks is not an encyclopaedia, but a user-friendly handbook that will hopefully inspire you to cook better than ever, as well as encourage a sense of adventure and discovery. In addition to the many hundreds of ideas provided in the descriptions of individual ingredients, the book includes more than 70 illustrated recipes. I have been hugely fortunate to be able to use, alongside my own recipes, selected recipe contributions from a handful of the world's most famous and talented cooks, chefs and restaurateurs. Many of these are colleagues, friends and my own food heroes. To them, for their faith in this project and their generous good wishes, I say a special thank you.

At the back of the book is a list of suppliers, which includes many of my favourite sources of the ingredients featured in *Food for Cooks*.

We have had the good luck to live, for two decades, in the middle of one of London's most delectable food locations: Notting Hill. To be surrounded by extraordinarily good delis, spice merchants, ethnic grocers, traditional, rare-breed and halal butchers, bakers, *charcutiers*, *pâtissiers*, fishmongers, cheesemongers and specialist food suppliers, let alone the exuberant stall holders of Portobello Road market, is an enduring joy and a constant education.

Cheers and *bon appétit!*

Clare Ferguson

savoury
flavourings

whole spices

Spices are the tawny treasures of the kitchen, capable of transforming our meals into something stupendous. They are the seeds, fruits, berries, buds, flowers, bark, roots or rhizomes of certain plants that become intensely aromatic when dried or preserved. Their heady aroma emanates from volatile essential oils that become concentrated within the spice as it dries. Once a whole spice is crushed, the oils are released and quickly evaporate into the atmosphere, so it is usually best to buy the whole spice rather than its ground counterpart. And it is important to grind spices only when you are ready to cook. Many spices can, of course, be used in sweet dishes, but most are used more often in savoury preparations.

1 Peppercorns The essential kitchen spice, peppercorns come in various guises. Black peppercorns (a) are picked as unripe berries, which are then sun-dried. The white peppercorn (b) is the same berry, only riper and with the outer layer removed. White pepper is very mild and offers heat rather than flavour. Green peppercorns (c), unripe berries from the same plant, are available brined, pickled or dried. These work well in steak sauces, or crushed in seasoning mixes.

Pink (or red) peppercorns (d), which come from a different plant, are used for spiciness and colourfulness rather than hotness. Chinese Sichuan (or Szechuan) peppercorns (e) are fragrant, but not incendiary. Toast and then grind them, and use in coatings or in fried dishes with fish or chicken.

2 Mustard seeds Tiny perfect spheres, mustard seeds come in black, brown and white. Black mustard seeds (a) are hard to harvest and are nowadays often replaced by brown, which are less pungent. White mustard seeds (b) are more bitter and have strong preservative powers. They are useful in vinegars, for pickling. The hot mustard oil that the seeds contain emerges only once they are wetted.

storage

Buy spices little and often, use them quickly and, above all, ditch them once they fade in taste and smell – probably after about six months. Store them, airtight, in a cool, dark and dry place: a larder or drawer is perfect, a spice rack next to your cooker is not. Use dark glass, china or metal containers, and label them with the date of purchase.

3 Juniper berries These plump berries are sweet and pungent, and enrich game, such as venison or partridge, pork pâtés and potato dishes. Squash the berries to a paste or lightly crush before use.

4 Cinnamon bark or sticks The intense aroma of cinnamon excels in both savoury and sweet dishes. Superbly versatile, it finds a home in everything from casseroles to coffee, and in numerous spice mixes, from apple pie mix to garam masala. In Europe, it is a popular ingredient for baking, while in the Middle East it is essential in many lamb dishes.

5 Saffron The dried stigmas of the *Crocus sativus* plant are the world's costliest spice. When dried into fragile threads, saffron has an intense, musky odour that is vital in dishes such as paella, bouillabaisse and biriani. Syrups, glazes, cakes and icings also taste and look gorgeous with saffron added. Always use saffron in tiny amounts: too much can repel. Add it late in cooking, either soaked in a liquid or crushed (see page 16).

6 Nutmeg with mace When freshly grated, this aromatic seed has a pungent, warming taste. It is useful in both savoury and sweet cooking, whether it's in cheese dishes or apple puddings. Try to buy nutmeg that still has its red, web-like outer layer, or mace, which is similar in flavour to nutmeg, but mellower.

7 Cloves The tongue-numbing flavour of these dried buds makes it ideal for pickle-making, but offensive if used in large quantities. With its long end, the clove is perfect for stabbing into a peeled onion for scenting stock or bread sauce, or into the fat of a joint of ham. Cloves taste good with apple, or pound them up with sugar and cinnamon to make a fruit crumble spice mix.

8 Star anise This woody seed head contains shiny red-brown and highly perfumed seeds. Spicy but bitter, the crushed or whole heads or seeds enliven many Chinese dishes. For a quick aromatic fruit salad, make a sugar-based syrup (see page 44) and add a few whole heads, along with cinnamon and vanilla.

9 Fenugreek seeds These hard seeds are most useful in spice mixes, and are a vital ingredient in curry powder (see page 13). Also used in pickles, fenugreek needs gentle heat to bring out its scent.

10 Cumin seeds The cumin seed has a powerful, slightly aniseedy taste which can easily dominate a dish. Often combined with chilli and coriander, it is vital in many spice mixes, including garam masala. Crushed, it adds savour to braised meats and baked fish.

11 Cardamom seeds These have a deliciously pungent, eucalyptus-like flavour. Normally, the green pods are simply crushed in order to remove the aromatic black seeds, and then discarded. Cardamom is common in curries, but is also good in desserts, such as apple tart and rice pudding.

12 Fennel seeds These pale seeds add a subtle aniseedy, celery-like flavour to food. They are great in spiced or fish stews, breads or herb and spice seasoning mixes. They can be substituted for dill seeds.

13 Coriander seeds Often used in Thai, Indian and Pakistani dishes, coriander seeds give an intensely fragrant burst of woody, orange spiciness, which suits both savoury and sweet foods. Teamed with chilli and cumin, coriander is superb in curries. Crushed with salt and cumin, coriander is good rubbed into poultry, pork, fish and lamb.

14 Caraway seeds These have a warm, biting but sweet piquancy, and work wonders in rye breads, cakes and biscuits. Pounded together with coarse sugar, caraway is good on bread and butter.

15 Vanilla pods These cured tropical pods produce a sweet and magically fragrant flavour. Good-quality vanilla pods are plump, glossy and supple, and have a strong scent. Both the pod and the fine black gummy seed paste inside can be used (see page 16) to add a sublime flavour to custards and other sweet dishes.

A pod can be reused (simply wash it and dry it), though its flavour will be weakened.

ground spices

While a spice's aroma will gradually diminish and fade (due to the spice's increased surface area) once ground, certain pre-ground spices are useful when a fine powder is required – in cakes and savoury sauces, for example – or for convenience when there's no time to grind your own. This applies particularly to spice mixes, which can be time-devouring to make; furthermore, the recipes of even the most standard mixes can vary. However, you can have fun creating your own simple mixes: spices mixed with salt or sugar can be sprinkled on all manner of foods.

1 Turmeric The dried and ground rhizome of the turmeric plant is essential to most curries, and is also useful in pickles and marinades. Or add it to oil, butter, ghee or stock to flavour (and colour) noodles, rice and root vegetable dishes. Never overdo it, use it raw, or substitute it for saffron.

2 Ginger Dried, ground ginger – pale, pungent and sweet – is more versatile than its fresh parent. It is useful for baking, and also in syrups, glazes and batters. Dust some over fish before sautéing, or rub it over pork or chicken instead of flour before cooking. Pounded together, ginger, cinnamon, peppercorns and salt make a pungent seasoning.

3 Ground pepper Coarsely ground black pepper (pictured) is useful when making batter, dough or pastry, or for quick coatings, while the invisibility of white pepper makes it perfect if you want spotless cheese sauces, cream-based reductions or pastries.

4 Cinnamon Since grinding cinnamon bark to a fine powder requires serious time and effort, it is better to buy ground cinnamon for using in cakes, biscuits and other sweet dishes. Use it in glazes, in spiced butters, or mix it with sugar and sprinkle it over peaches, muffins or buttered toast.

5 Paprika Made from a type of hot red chilli pepper, this ground spice can vary in its flavour and pungency. The best-quality paprikas are vivid red and have a soft, fruity hotness: this is one spice that you can use by the tablespoonful. Use it in meat and poultry dishes (it is essential in Hungarian goulash), in mayonnaise and in dressings.

6 Chilli powder The colour, flavour and power of chilli powder varies according to which type of chilli is used (see pages 17–18). For the best results, grind your own from dried chillies. Substitute Tabasco sauce, cayenne pepper or hot paprika if necessary.

7 Cayenne pepper This is made, like paprika, from a type of hot red chilli pepper, but is considerably hotter. Just a pinch gives a desirable, rosy hotness to mayonnaises, dressings, vinaigrettes, bastes and rubs for roasts and barbecued meats, as well as being useful in curries, chilli con carne and spice pastes. Substitute chilli powder (which is similar but usually coarser) or dried, crumbled chilli if necessary.

8 Annatto (achiote) This mildly earthy, warm, orange-red powder, made commercially by grinding fiendishly hard annatto seeds, is used, above all, to provide colour: cheeses such as Red Leicester contain annatto, and it is also used to dye kippers.

It is essential for some Mexican and Indian spice mixes. Otherwise, use it in dry rubs, in marinades, syrups or glazes. You can even use it to colour rice, pasta or grain dishes. Annatto is also available as a paste.

mixes

1 Dukkah (du'a) An Egyptian mix of toasted spices, seeds and nuts, dukkah is delicious as a topping or garnish. The contents can vary, but often includes sesame seeds, coriander, cumin, cinnamon, peanuts and dried mint. Try dipping some torn flatbread first into good olive oil and then into dukkah: delicious.

2 Cajun spice mix This Louisiana spice mix flatters the bold, spicy tastes of New Orleans cooking. A typical Cajun mix includes black pepper, cayenne, cinnamon, cumin, thyme, oregano, dried garlic and green filé powder (the stuff that gives gumbo its body). To make your own, see page 14.

3 Ras-el-hanout Many tagines and other meat, vegetable and fish dishes are improved by this euphorically scented spice mix from North Africa. It may have anything from 20 to 100 ingredients: a typical mix includes everything from cardamom and cayenne pepper to citrus peel and dried rose buds. Use it rubbed over poultry, fish, meat or game before cooking, or heat it in oil, butter or ghee and mix with liquids before adding other ingredients.

4 Chinese five-spice The warm, mildly liquorice scentedness of this spice mix gives an unmistakably Chinese flavour. The five spices involved are: star anise, cassia (or cinnamon), Sichuan peppercorns, cloves and fennel seeds. The mix is superb with pork – try it in a sweet, soy sauce-based glaze for roasted pork fillet.

5 Zataar (zathar) This Middle Eastern mix usually contains two parts thyme (or oregano) to one part sumac (see page 26), sometimes with sesame seeds added. It is great when sprinkled on lightly oiled flatbreads and then baked, or mixed into garlicky soft cheese. In butter or oil, it tastes good drizzled over poultry or vegetables before baking or roasting.

6 Garam masala Common in northern Indian cooking, but used worldwide, garam masala's hotness and spiciness may vary, along with the ingredients: black pepper, cumin, cardamom, cinnamon and nutmeg are normally included. Use garam masala in spicy stews and curries, lentil and bean dishes, or to sprinkle over flatbreads before baking.

7 Japanese seven-spice seasoning The seven 'spices' in this tasty mix (also known as *shichimi togarashi*) are: red chilli flakes, sansho (Sichuan pepper or prickly ash berries), sesame seeds, nori (seaweed) flakes, dried mandarin peel, hemp seeds and white poppy seeds.

Available in hot, medium and mild strengths, this spice mix can be used to season fish and seafood, chicken, noodle and rice dishes, as well as leafy salads and delicately cooked vegetables. It makes a very pretty condiment for rice and noodles.

8 Curry powder A European rather than an Indian invention dating back to the colonial period, ready-mixed curry powder is despised by purists. However, it is extremely popular in Britain, France and Scandinavia, and is surprisingly versatile, being useful in anything from a Malay fish curry to an Indian vindaloo. Use it, also, in pickles, mayonnaises, and in kedgeree.

In India, a more authentic version of curry powder is garam masala (see above).

chermoula spice paste

Makes 300g

This vivid Moroccan paste is delicious spread over
fish, meat or poultry before baking. Simply whiz up
these ingredients in a food processor: 4 crushed
garlic cloves, 2 crumbled bay leaves, 1 small bunch
thyme (stems removed), 2 teaspoons mild paprika,
1 teaspoon cayenne pepper, 1 teaspoon ground
cumin, 4 tablespoons chopped pickled lemon peel,
a handful each of fresh coriander and flat-leaf parsley
(chopped), juice of 1 lemon, and 6 tablespoons olive
oil. This quantity is plenty for 2 large fish, 4 lamb
shanks or 8 chicken legs. Store any extra in the
freezer (using an ice cube tray) for 30 days.

colombo spice mix

Makes 180g

Originally from East India, this spice mix is now used
worldwide. Pan-toast, cool and combine 1 tablespoon
each of cumin seeds, coriander seeds, brown mustard
seeds, black peppercorns and rock salt crystals. Add
3 tablespoons coconut flakes and 2 teaspoons each
of crushed chilli flakes, ground turmeric and ground
ginger. Coarsely grind. Pan-toast 2 tablespoons long-
grain white rice until it colours and pops. Cool, crush
and add it to the spices. Use the spice mix to coat
fish or meat, then cook in coconut milk and stock,
adding garlic and onion to taste. Or, sizzle the spice
mix, garlic and onion in ghee, butter or oil, then add
the remaining ingredients.

cajun spice mix

Makes 75g (or enough for 10 servings)

Combine 2 teaspoons each of black peppercorns,
fennel seeds and dried oregano, sage and thyme. Add
1 teaspoon each of rock salt, cumin seeds, paprika,
cayenne and mustard powder. Grind everything
together. At the time of use, rub the spice mix over
meat, poultry or game, using 2 tablespoons for
about 500g of food. Sauté the coated meat in butter,
corn oil or lard with 1 sliced onion and 2 cloves
chopped garlic, then stew or casserole as needed.
If chargrilling, barbecuing or grilling, rub the spice mix
in, adding the onion and garlic (reduced to a purée)
at the same time.

scented sugar

Makes about 150g

Crush together 2 tablespoons each of caraway
seeds, cardamom pods and crumbled cinnamon sticks
using a pestle and mortar, and add 4 tablespoons
granulated sugar. Continue to grind and pound until
you achieve a good blend. This is luscious when
sprinkled over slices of melon, pineapple, apples,
pears or halved bananas, wrapped in foil, and then
grilled. The scented sugar will keep well in an airtight
jar in a cool place.

yucatecan achiote seasoning paste

Authentic Mexican, a fascinating book by Rick Bayless with Deann Groen Bayless, explores the rich, earthy flavours of that cuisine and has been a huge inspiration in the popularity of traditional Mexican cooking in the United States. This recipe shows one aspect of the use of local spices for which the food of Mexico is renowned.

Makes: ½ cup, about 100g

Ingredients

1 tbsp achiote (annatto) seeds
1 tsp black peppercorns (or scant
   1½ tsp ground)
1 tsp dried oregano
4 cloves (or ⅛ tsp ground)
½ tsp cumin seeds (or generous
   ½ tsp ground)
2.5cm cinnamon stick (or 1 tsp
   ground)
1 tsp coriander seeds (or
   generous 1 tsp ground)
1 scant tsp salt
5 garlic cloves, peeled
2 tbsp cider vinegar
1½ tsp flour

Method

1. Measure the achiote seeds, peppercorns, oregano, cloves, cumin, cinnamon and coriander seeds into an electric grinder and pulverise as completely as possible; it will take a minute or more, due to the hardness of the achiote. Transfer to a small bowl and mix with the salt.
2. Finely mince the garlic, then sprinkle it with some of the spice mixture and use the back of a spoon or a flexible spreader to work it back and forth, smearing it into a smooth paste. Scrape this into the remaining spice powder, then mix in the vinegar and flour.
3. Scoop the paste into a small jar, cover and let it stand for several hours (or, preferably, overnight) before using.

This is delicious rubbed all over 15g chunks of chicken. Wrap them in wetted banana leaf strips and secure with wooden cocktail sticks. Bake in an oven preheated to 200°C/Gas 6 for 20–30 minutes or microwave on High for 5–6 minutes, or until firm and fragrant. Unwrap and eat.

using spices

Whole spices usually need treating in order to release the oils that produce their aroma: whether by grinding, pounding or 'bruising' (crushing); by pan-toasting, which enhances the flavour of small seeds, such as coriander or cumin, before grinding; or by dissolving or heating in a liquid, whether it's oil, alcohol, stock, syrup or just water. While most whole spices are added at the start of a recipe to allow time for their flavour to flood out, ground spices can be added late in the cooking.

Grinding spices
The best way to grind by hand is to use a medium-sized ceramic pestle and mortar with an unglazed surface. For speed, it is also worth investing in an electric spice (or coffee) grinder, which should be dedicated to the purpose. If you are grinding only small amounts, adding sugar or salt provides more friction. Should you be short of equipment, a rolling pin or a hammer make rudimentary tools for grinding and crushing.

Using a vanilla pod
Split the pod lengthways with a sharp knife and add it to milk or cream as it heats. Leave the liquid to infuse for 20–30 minutes before removing the pod. For a more intense flavour, scrape out the seedy paste with the tip of a knife, scrape this on to sugar lumps and whisk into already heated milk, or whichever liquid your recipe specifies; add the pod, too, if you wish, but remove it before finishing the dish.

Pan-toasting or dry-frying spices
Place the spices, such as cumin seeds, in a preheated heavy-based frying pan or wok, without any oil. Stir or shake continuously over a moderate to high heat for 1–3 minutes, until the seeds start to become aromatic and change colour. Don't worry if they start to pop, but make sure that they don't burn. Cool, transfer to a cold surface, grind and use as needed.

Tempering spices
In India, tempered spices (that is, sizzled in hot oil) are poured over certain dishes, just before serving. Heat several tablespoons of an appropriate oil in a heavy-based pan. Add the spices – such as mustard seeds, chopped fresh ginger, dried crumbled red chilli and turmeric powder – and sauté for 5 seconds. Add lemon juice, salt and a splash of water. Pour over plain rice, noodles or lentils: superb.

Preparing saffron
First, lightly toast a pinch of saffron threads on a piece of aluminium foil, or in a frying pan, over low heat. Then crush them to a powder using a pestle and mortar or the flat side of a knife: adding coarse salt or sugar can make this easier. For easier assimilation into the dish, dissolve the threads in a few tablespoons of hot water (or rum or vodka) for a few minutes – watch the colour flood out.

nine-spice rack of lamb with cucumber relish

This recipe, from *Cooking at Home with a Four-Star Chef* by Jean-Georges Vongerichten, shows the celebrated chef-restaurateur's trademark French-Asian influences. His dishes, though sophisticated, are simple and bold. He says: "You can use this spice rub with any cut of lamb (or beef, for that matter: it's great on grilled steak), but small racks (of lamb) are easy and festive. And the crispy chops are sensational set off against the cool relish."

Serves 4

Ingredients

1 tsp cardamom seeds
1 tsp sesame seeds
1 tsp fenugreek seeds
2.5cm piece of cinnamon stick
1 clove
1 tsp cumin seeds
½ tsp dried chilli flakes
½ nutmeg, smashed into a couple of chunks with the side of a cleaver
1 tsp ground mace
1 cucumber
salt and freshly ground black pepper
12–15 mint leaves
4 × 3–rib racks of lamb
1 tsp peanut or other oil

Method

1. Preheat the oven to 250°C/Gas 10 (or your oven's highest temperature). Combine the spices in a dry skillet and toast over medium-high heat, shaking the pan frequently, until the mixture starts to smoke and becomes aromatic (about 2 minutes). Grind the spices together in a coffee or spice grinder; stop before the mixture becomes powdery – it should have the texture of coarsely ground, even cracked, black pepper. ('You can store this mixture in an opaque, covered container for up to a year.')

2. Peel the cucumber, cut it in half and scoop out the seeds. Cut into 2.5cm sections (the size is not critical), sprinkle with salt and toss together with the mint. Transfer to a food processor and blend, stopping the machine to scrape down the mixture once or twice, until finely minced but not puréed. Place in a strainer but don't press to remove all the liquid; the relish should remain moist.

3. Cut little X's in the fat of the racks of lamb; this allows it to become extra crisp. Season with salt and pepper, then sprinkle all over with the spice mixture.

4. Heat a large ovenproof frying pan over high heat for about 2 minutes. Add the oil, swirl it around the pan, and pour it out so that only a film of oil is left. Brown the lamb on the meaty side for 2 minutes, then on the bony side for 1 minute. Turn the lamb on the meaty side again and place the frying pan in the oven. Roast for 8 minutes for very rare, 10 minutes for rare, 12 minutes for medium-rare to medium. Serve the racks with a scoop of the relish on the side.

dried herbs

Thanks to global trade, many herbs are now available fresh all year round, so the need to buy the dried varieties is much reduced. Moreover, soft-leaved herbs such as basil and coriander are useless when dried. Certain robust and strong-flavoured herbs dry well, however, and in some cases are even better dried than fresh. Home-dried herbs, especially wild herbs, often keep the best intensity: hang bunches, upside down, in a sunny window or over a breezy doorway, until brittle, and then crush or crumble at the time of use. Store dried herbs airtight, and discard them after six months, or when they start to lose their pungency.

1 Lavender With its pungent, sweet scent, lavender can be delicious in herb mixes or when used to scent syrups and vinegars; lavender-infused white wine vinegar is great for dressings. Also, ground with granulated sugar to a mauve powder, it is delicious in ice cream, or on baked stone fruits.

2 Thyme Heavily fragrant, thyme comes in hundreds of varieties. Even commercially dried thyme is aromatic, giving off an earthy aroma with hints of lemon, camphor and mint. It is splendidly versatile: superb in thick soups, stocks, stews, marinades and stuffings; great with meat, poultry and game; and perfect teamed with garlic, onion or tomatoes.

3 Curry leaves Used regularly by Pakistani and Indian cooks, curry leaves have a slightly bitter but appealing curryish, citrussy taste.

They are good in Asian stocks, soups and curries, but suit Western cooking, too. The flavour of the leaves often comes out when they are tempered (see page 16). Dried leaves are vital for some spice mixes: try grinding dried curry leaves with coriander and cumin seeds, sea salt and pink peppercorns as a seasoning.

4 Sage A powerfully fragrant herb, sage comes in several varieties of differing intensity. It has a camphor-like and almost medicinal taste, which cuts richness and goes well with pork, duck, goose, lamb or bacon, and also excels in stuffings, cheesy toppings, sauces and soups.

5 Rosemary The strong woody-resinous taste of rosemary survives drying fairly well. The leaves, however, become quite hard and spiky, and should be removed from a dish before

serving. Rosemary is excellent in gravies and marinades for chicken, lamb and other meats. It combines well with thyme and lemon.

6 Oregano This herb is essential to Greek and Italian cooking, where cooks use it with everything from pizza and pasta to grilled meats. Its biting pepperiness and penetrating flavour ripen as it cooks, so use the herb cautiously. Good-quality dried oregano is excellent and lasts for ages.

7 Bay This elegant, spicy herb, with its medicinal and sweetly peppery tones, is more often used dried than fresh, and is essential in every kitchen. Bay leaves underpin French haute cuisine, being used to scent béchamel sauce, stocks, marinades and tomato sauces. Pounded together with sugar to a powder, bay leaves scent custards and ice creams superbly.

using dried herbs

Dried herbs must be used differently from their fresh counterparts. For example, they are often best used when cooked, or else need a long soak in the cooking juices for the flavour to come out. Dry-frying dried herbs in advance can sometimes help coax out extra flavour, and they can work well in herb-spice mixes, pounded together with sugar or sea salt. One teaspoon of dried herbs is usually roughly equivalent to one tablespoon of fresh.

greek salad with herbs

This superb salad, famous in Greece, is contributed by Mediterranean food writer Rena Salaman, whose book, *Greek Food,* is a real classic. Tomato salad is the summer salad *par excellence* in Greece, almost always dressed with plain olive oil and never with vinaigrette. When white feta cheese is added, the salad is known as *horiatiki*; this is often served in tavernas.

Serves 2–3

Ingredients

225g tomatoes
1 onion, thinly sliced
1 green pepper, cored and thinly sliced
½ cucumber, peeled and thinly sliced
100g Greek feta cheese, sliced (optional)
12–16 black olives, such as Kalamata (optional)
3–4 tbsp extra virgin olive oil
salt and freshly ground black pepper
dried oregano, crumbled

Method

1. Rinse the tomatoes. Cut them in half and slice into thin quarters.
2. If you want to reduce the sharpness of the onion, soak the slices in a little salted water for 5–10 minutes, then take out and squeeze gently. Combine with the tomatoes, green pepper and cucumber.
3. Add the feta and the olives, if using. Dress the salad with the olive oil, salt, black pepper and a sprinkle of oregano.

salts

Salt, or sodium chloride, is essential for life, and is one of the five basic tastes. It can radically alter the taste of food, bringing out the flavour of other ingredients or counteracting sweetness. It exists either as sea salt or rock salt. The former can be mass-produced artificially by the boiling and evaporation of sea water, but the best kinds are obtained by letting sea water evaporate naturally. Rock salt, found in crystalline deposits below ground (the remains of petrified prehistoric seas), is a less intriguing product than sea salt and can have a more minerally taste.

According to its provenance or processing, salt can vary in flavour, colour, coarseness and purity, as well as in 'saltiness'. Natural sea salts, for example, may contain traces of other minerals that can affect both the flavour and colour. The costliest sea salt crystals are best used sparingly, sprinkled over a tomato salad, or served as a condiment, but most coarse salt is used for cooking. Common table salt is usually made from finely ground rock salt, with anti-caking substances added to keep it free-flowing.

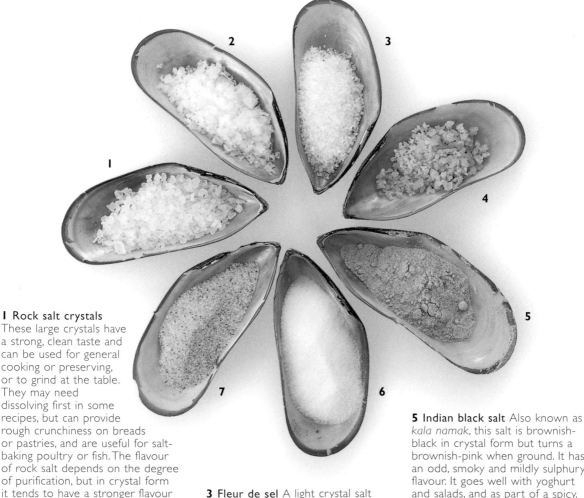

1 Rock salt crystals
These large crystals have a strong, clean taste and can be used for general cooking or preserving, or to grind at the table. They may need dissolving first in some recipes, but can provide rough crunchiness on breads or pastries, and are useful for salt-baking poultry or fish. The flavour of rock salt depends on the degree of purification, but in crystal form it tends to have a stronger flavour than sea salt.

2 Maldon sea salt These highly desirable, flaky crystals, produced in Essex, England, are sea-flavoured, clean, and without bitterness, and are easily crushable under the tongue, between the fingers or with a pestle and mortar. They dissolve easily, and only a small amount is needed to give an instant hit of saltiness. While too expensive for bulk cooking, the flakes can give a delicate crunch to anything from grilled fish to soft-cooked vegetables.

3 Fleur de sel A light crystal salt from France, *fleur de sel* is the most exclusive of the naturally dried sea salts, being scooped off the surface of the crystallising pools before the wind or rain disperses it.

4 Gros sel (sel gris) These opaque crystals from the Guérande, in Brittany, are formed naturally, but are scraped from lower down than *fleur de sel*. They may contain other minerals and trace elements, such as calcium and magnesium, which contribute to the colour and delicious taste.

5 Indian black salt Also known as *kala namak*, this salt is brownish-black in crystal form but turns a brownish-pink when ground. It has an odd, smoky and mildly sulphury flavour. It goes well with yoghurt and salads, and as part of a spicy, peppery sprinkle.

6 Fine sea salt Artificially produced sea salt, finely ground, is useful in most ways that sea salt crystals are, but is more convenient. It may lack the crunch of crystals, but it is free from the slightly bitter taste of standard table salt.

7 Celery salt Flavoured with dried celery leaves or celery seeds, this salt is useful rubbed over fish or poultry, in sandwiches, breads or muffins, or in Bloody Mary cocktails.

salt-crusted sea bass with green herb dressing

A layer of salt under and over a whole fish, which insulates as it bakes, lets the fish steam-cook gently. The resulting fish is not salty at all, just succulent.

Serves 4

Ingredients
1 small lemon, sliced (optional)
4 sprigs each of thyme, bay and parsley
2 tsp black peppercorns, roughly crushed
1 sea bass (about 1kg), gutted, cleaned, with scales left on
500g rock salt crystals

Method
1. Select a large porcelain baking dish or metal roasting pan in which the fish fits snugly. (The larger the dish, the more salt will be required.)
2. Put the lemon slices (optional), the herb sprigs and peppercorns into the fish's gut cavity. Use cocktail sticks to secure the belly flaps closed.
3. Spread a layer of salt about 2cm deep over the base of the baking dish. Set the fish on top and pour another layer of salt all over it, patting the crystals down firmly so that there are no gaps; dampening the salt a little can help the process.
4. Bake in an oven preheated to 200°C/Gas 6 for 30–40 minutes, or until the edges of the gills, curled and splayed outwards, become visible through the salt, and you can smell a delicious, fishy aroma.
5. Take the fish to the table and invite your diners to tap and then peel away the salt crust, scales and skin to reveal the silky flesh underneath. Serve with crusty, white bread, lemon halves and melted butter or the green herb dressing described below.

green herb dressing

Ingredients
2 large handfuls of flat-leaf parsley, tightly packed (50g)
1 large handful mint or tarragon sprigs, tightly packed (30g)
6 spring onions, roughly chopped
4–6 garlic cloves, crushed in their skins, then peeled
2 tbsp freshly squeezed lemon juice
8 tbsp melted butter

Method
1. Combine the first three ingredients in a food processor and whiz for about 30 seconds, until roughly blended.
2. Add the remaining ingredients and whiz again to make a thick sauce. Any extra, unused sauce can be refrigerated for up to 2 days. This sauce is also good with eggs, potatoes or rice.

vinegars

A popular condiment and preservative for millennia, vinegar, with its distinctively sharp taste, is a result of the natural process of fermentation of alcohol to acetic acid. It is made all over the world, often based on the favourite local drink, whether it's wine in France, or rice wine in the Far East.

The best vinegars are those made from wine (or grape must, used to make balsamic vinegar), though not all wine vinegars are of good quality: to make above-average sherry vinegar or red wine vinegar, for example, you must start off with high-quality liquor and use the slow, traditional Orléans process of production, which results in a smoother taste and preserves the flavour of the original wine. These good-quality wine vinegars are delicious used in dressings, to deglaze the pan after cooking roast meats, or swirled into butter as a simple sauce. They are also poles apart from rapid-production wine vinegars, which are made in as little as 24 hours. Cheap, distinctive vinegars such as malt vinegar, produced commercially from beers and ales, are best left for pickling, or for dishes where strength is more important than flavour.

Lots of bad wine vinegars claim to be 'produced in the traditional way', so it is more reliable to judge a vinegar by its cost and other information on the label: good vinegars do not contain colourings. If you do end up with a poor vinegar, adding leftover port, sherry or wine can soften the harshness, as can diluting it with a little water.

1 Red and white wine vinegars Traditionally, the source of many wine vinegars was the Loire region of France, but today excellent wine vinegars are made all over the world, from Spain to California.

The best wine vinegars usually specify which wine they are made from, and echo that wine's flavour. Red wine vinegar (a), made from Rioja, for example, gives an oaky and full-bodied vinegar, while a white wine vinegar made from Riesling is elegantly scented. White wine vinegar is milder than red, and is more often used for making flavoured vinegars – by adding anything from chillies to seaweed;

tarragon-flavoured vinegar (b) is particularly successful. (It is easy to flavour your own vinegar: just add the herb or spice and let it infuse for a few days.)

All these vinegars are good for all culinary and table uses, whether it's in vinaigrettes, marinades, steak sauces or fresh fruit chutneys.

2 Sherry vinegar At its best, this nutty, aromatic and often punchy vinegar, from Jerez in Spain, has much of the character of the original sherry: vinegar made from oloroso, for example, can be superb. Sherry vinegar is great with offal and foie gras, and in gazpacho

or white or green bean salads. Deglaze the pan with some when sautéing seafood, or drizzle some into a dressing for warm potato salad.

3 Cider vinegar This mild and fruity vinegar, with relatively low acidity, is produced in cider-making communities such as Normandy, and is very popular in the United States. The flavour varies according to the type of apple used.

Cider vinegar works well with pork (deglaze the pan with it after roasting the meat), in tomato or fruit sauces, in barbecue marinades, or in simple herb vinaigrettes.

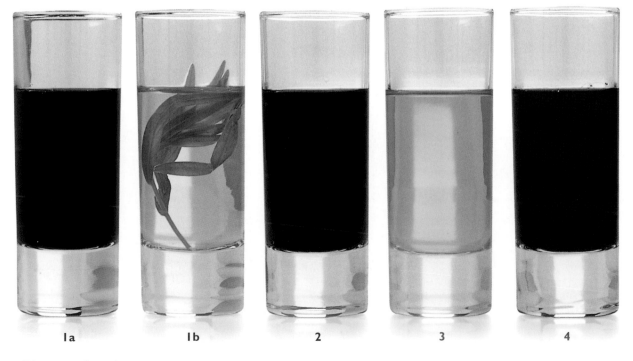

| 1a | 1b | 2 | 3 | 4 |

4 Red fruit vinegars Fruit vinegars can be made by fermenting the actual fruit juices, but most commonly are made by simply macerating the fruit in wine vinegar. Fruits like raspberries and black-currants seem to perform best. Avoid buying bottles with fruit still inside – it looks nice but can cause cloudiness.

Use red fruit vinegar with duck and other rich meats, in dressings, glazes and fruit purées, or sprinkle it over leafy salads and fresh fruits.

5 Balsamic vinegar Identifying a good balsamic vinegar, which differs from other wine vinegars because it is made from must rather than from wine, is a minefield. At its best, balsamic vinegar is a wonderful, fragrant, sharp, rich brown syrup that is good enough to drink straight as a liqueur.

If you can find it, or afford it, buy aged balsamic vinegar from the Modena or Reggio provinces in Italy, which is labelled 'tradizionale' and has a distinctive seal to show that it conforms to certain (high) standards. This is aged for 12 years or more and is so expensive that it is best used only as a condiment, trickled over bitter-leaved salads or strawberries and other ripe fruits.

Vinegar labelled 'artisanale' has not been matured for as long as tradizionale has, but it is often good, though with less complex flavours. It costs considerably less, and can be used more liberally, in vinaigrettes and reductions.

At the bottom of the scale is the industrial-level condiment,

which is made very quickly. It may be 'made traditionally', but a glance at the label is likely to show that it contains additives. If you buy this grade, boiling the vinegar down until it is reduced by half can produce a better flavour.

6 Malt vinegar This everyday brown vinegar, usually darkened with caramel, is malty but not subtle. Use it for pickling where colour does not matter, or in robust, earthy dishes, spicy sauces, tomato chutney or relishes to eat with strong cheeses. This is the traditional vinegar to sprinkle over fish and chips.

7 Distilled vinegar Concentrated by distillation, this crystal-clear, fiercely sharp malt vinegar (also known as 'white' or 'spirit' vinegar) is convenient when the malty taste or brown colour of ordinary malt vinegar is inappropriate, and when intensity matters – for pearl onion pickles or crunchy dill pickles, for example. Distilled vinegar is a useful acidifier, in fresh mint sauce, or to mix with hot mustard, and can also be used in spicy Southeast Asian dishes. It should be used in tiny amounts, or diluted.

8 Rice vinegar Both Japan and China make vinegars fermented from rice wine. These vinegars can vary a great deal in taste and colour (white, brown and black rice are all used), but they are generally clear and light-flavoured, and sweeter and less acidic than many of the vinegars made in Europe. Perhaps not surprisingly, they are well suited to rice dishes.

Japanese white rice vinegar (a) has a mild but tart, clean taste. It is essential for flavouring the rice for sushi, and gives a pleasant flavour to dressings, creamy sauces and delicate, sweetish glazes for fish and seafood. It may come flavoured, with herbs, chillies, sesame seeds, or even bonito shavings.

Chinese white rice vinegar (b) tends to be sharper than its Japanese equivalent but is also good in rice or noodle dishes, or in glazes for fish and seafood. Chinese brown rice vinegar is fruitier and fuller-flavoured, and is useful for marinades or dressings. More striking, though, is China's inky black rice vinegar, which is mellow and sweet, and works well in highly caramelised, long-cooked pork or duck dishes.

storage

The high acid level in vinegar means that it keeps well, for at least six months and usually much longer. Store your bottles in a cool, dark place, particularly those containing vinegars that you use only occasionally. Since vinegar's acetic acid corrodes, never store it for any period of time in containers with metal tops; plastic, ceramic or cork is safer.

5   6   7   8a   8b

souring agents

In addition to naturally sour fruit juices, wines and vinegars, a range of other natural and man-made substances can help create the necessary sharp taste for certain foods and drinks, as well as act as a preservative. This group of sometimes delicious, sometimes intense substances is often neglected and should be present in any cook's pantry.

1 Verjuice 'Green juice' – the juice of unripe sour fruit (usually grapes) – is useful when the sharpness of lemon or vinegar would be too aggressive. Use it as a dressing with greens, or to give extra depth to marinades, stocks, sauces and even cocktails.

2 Acetic acid 33% ($C_2H_4O_2$) This acidic liquid (a concentrate of the active ingredient in vinegar) is useful for making gherkin or cucumber pickles. It must be stored in a cool, dark place (**away from children's reach**), and diluted 1:2 with water before use. Wash your hands after using it. Good chemists should stock acetic acid.

3 Tamarind paste This sticky paste (or concentrate) is made from the pods of the tamarind tree, and is the most common souring agent in Indian and Southeast Asian cooking. With a delicious, rounded sour taste, it is great in curries, soups and many chicken or meat dishes. It is also available as a sauce.

4 Amchoor (amchur) A sweet-sour, aromatic powder, produced in India by grinding up dried, unripe mangoes, amchoor has a lovely astringent taste accompanied by a sweetish tang. It tastes delicious added to curries, chutneys and pickles, and works well in stews, dhals and spice mixes.

5 Sumac This attractive powder, made from the seeds of the berry-like sumac fruit, imparts an agreeable fruity sourness to dishes. It is widely used in the Middle East, sprinkled on grilled fish, meat, or in spice mixes. Sumac balances the richness of, say, fatty lamb dishes, while also adding great colour.

6 Citric acid ($C_6H_8O_7$) If no lemon or orange juice is available, crystalline citric acid, diluted with hot water, can be used to replicate the taste. Use it to intensify sourness in drinks, or to help sharpen marinades. It is available from chemists.

7 Tartaric acid ($C_4H_6O_6$) Either powdery or crystalline, tartaric acid is the acidic ingredient in grapes and has a direct sour astringency. It serves a similar function to citric acid, but gives a grape taste rather than a lemony one.

8 Loomi (dried limes) In the Gulf States and Iran, loomi are used to sour rice pilaus and other dishes. They are fruity and sharp, and go well with cinnamon, ginger and cardamom, and with fresh herbs such as coriander. Leave them whole, or crush them before adding them to a dish, and then squeeze out and add the delicious pulp before serving. Or, crush and then grind them to sprinkle over or into savoury dishes.

9 Roselle (red sorrel) The fleshy, edible calyx of this plant gives a fruity, cranberry-like acidity to teas, cordials and preserves, as well as a powerful red pigmentation – hence its use in commercial red fruit teas.

barbecued quail in a fig bath

In this fascinating recipe, the Australian food writer Maggie Beer uses verjuice, which she produces herself, to brilliant effect. Maggie explains: "Steeping grilled quail in a fresh marinade is a technique I've long loved – the beauty of it is that the flavourings can be altered according to what you have to hand. Instead of dried figs, you could add grapes and roasted walnuts, or perhaps raisins that have been reconstituted in red wine vinegar and then tossed in nut-brown butter with some rosemary. A recipe is just an idea, after all."

Serves 4

Ingredients
8 quail
extra virgin olive oil
freshly ground black pepper

For the fig bath:
8 tiny white or 4 larger dried figs
verjuice
2 lemons
125ml extra virgin olive oil
40g basil leaves
freshly ground black pepper

Method
1. Using kitchen shears, cut away the backbone from each quail and slip out the rib cage with your fingers. Rub each bird with a little olive oil, then season with pepper and allow to sit for 1 hour before grilling.
2. Meanwhile, preheat a barbecue or prepare a fire, allowing the coals to burn down to glowing embers. Start to prepare the fig bath by soaking the figs for 20 minutes in enough verjuice to cover them, then drain and cut them in half (or quarters, if using larger figs).
3. Remove the zest from the lemons using a potato peeler, then juice 1 lemon. Set aside.
4. Grill the quail, turning them frequently, for about 8 minutes in all, depending on the heat of the fire.
5. While the quail are cooking, finish preparing the fig bath by pouring the olive oil into a shallow glass dish, then adding the figs, lemon zest and juice. Finely chop the basil and add it to the bath with a good grinding of pepper.
6. Transfer the cooked quail to the bath and let rest, turning once or twice, for 10 minutes, then serve with cracked wheat salad.

sauces

The global nature of our larders means that we can now use all manner of intriguing ready-made sauces to enliven dressings, stocks, soups, marinades, bastes or dipping sauces, as well as to use as condiments in their own right. Long-keeping, often ethnic, sauces are time- and effort-saving, and pleasingly diverse. Many oriental sauces are impossible to replicate at home, and are integral to Asian dishes, but note that some may contain additives such as colourings and flavour enhancers. Once opened, most sauces (unless they are high in natural preservatives, such as salt, acid, sugar or chillies) should be stored in a cool, dry place or else refrigerated.

1 Anchovy sauce This is available either as a sauce (or essence), or as a denser purée. Good versions are usually British or Italian, and add a flavoursome saltiness. A teaspoonful will season many creamy sauces, gravies, stocks and clear, Asian-style soups, and enhance minced beef, lamb or pork dishes. With shredded lemon rind, lemon juice and butter, it makes a wonderful seasoning for grills and seafood.

2 Mushroom ketchup Flavourful, intense and almost meaty, this dense liquid is not dissimilar to soy sauce. It can be used to enhance sauces, stocks, soups and stews (which may or may not contain mushrooms), and it works well in meat loaves, too.

3 Tomato ketchup The success of tomato ketchup is largely due to its natural sweetness, its texture and its vivid colour. Many people can't eat burgers or chips without it, but tomato ketchup is also useful for enhancing gravies or meat sauces. Combined with Worcestershire sauce, Tabasco sauce and garlic, it makes a mean barbecue baste.

4 Mole The ingredients in this famous Mexican sauce vary widely, but the constant is the presence of chilli pepper. Mole can be useful for pepping up marinades for meats and poultry, and, famously, can be combined with chocolate for rich Mexican dishes. You can create your own chocolate mole by simply heating a standard mole with dark chocolate, dried oregano and broth: this is good with poultry and game.

5 Mayonnaise Home-made mayonnaise is ambrosial, but it doesn't last. Commercial mayonnaise is not a gourmet food, but it does last. Try mixing it with chopped herbs, garlic, capers and gherkins, as a dressing; or with tarragon and tarragon vinegar, as a dressing for fish. Harissa folded through it makes a superb dip for tortilla chips. French, Belgian and American brands are often the best.

6 Salsa de tomatillo Made from tomatillos, a member of the Physalis (nightshade) family that resembles a small green tomato, this chilli- and garlic-enhanced salsa is essential in Mexican cooking. It is used in many tortilla-based dishes as a seasoning, spread or dipping sauce. Use it also with barbecued fish or pork, or with salty soft white cheese in leafy salads.

oriental sauces

1 Soy sauce (shoyu) This ancient Asian sauce is made from fermented soya beans, wheat and lots of salt. It is thin and obviously salty, with a varying rich and fruity sweetness. It comes either as 'dark' (a), which is sweet, heavy and rounded in flavour, or 'light' (b), which is thinner, paler and saltier. While the former is good for enriching marinades, stews and glazes, light soy is more versatile and is superb in stir-fries and meat, poultry and vegetable dishes. The 'naturally brewed' soy sauces have the greatest depth, but account for just one per cent of production.

A sweetened, thicker version of soy, called *kecap manis*, is made in Indonesia. Tamari is a Japanese soy made without wheat and popular for use with sushi and sashimi. Also look out for sauces that are based on soy, such as teriyaki and sukiyaki, both of which are good marinades.

2 Fish sauce Known as *nam pla* in Thailand, *nuoc mam* in Vietnam, and *patis* in the Filippines, fish sauce is an essential ingredient in these countries. Made from salted shrimp or fish, its clean, fresh saltiness enhances many dishes, and not necessarily seafood ones. Try it in stir-fried chicken dishes, with shrimp noodles, as part of a tomato relish, or in a sweet-and-sour sauce. Mixed with freshly squeezed lemon or lime juice and sliced chillies, it makes a wonderful Thai dipping sauce. The Japanese version of fish sauce is called *shotsura*.

3 Fermented black bean sauce This dark, sticky sauce can be very thick, medium-thick, crumbly or smoothly puréed. It is made from fermented, salted soya beans and is used in Southeast Asia and China. Black bean sauce is crucial with certain classic combinations, such as beef and vegetables with black beans, and shredded chicken, pork or duck with noodles; it is also used in crispy, deep-fried dumplings or steamed dim sum.

4 Plum sauce All sorts of variations exist, but this oriental sauce is often thin but sticky, and pinkish. Flavoured with fragments of plum, garlic and ginger, it can be used for spreading on Chinese pancakes to accompany glazed duck; added to stir-fries; or used in glazes and in sauces for cooked poultry dishes, often in combination with soy sauce.

5 Hoisin sauce This glossy, syrupy sauce is made from soy sauce and fermented black bean paste, chilli, star anise and other spices, and has a sweet-salt taste. It is mostly associated with Peking duck (warmed pancakes with shredded duck, cucumber and onions), but hoisin is a versatile product. It works well in vegetable, noodle and dumpling dishes, as well as with poultry, pork, beef and some seafood. Try diluting it with ginger wine and/or toasted sesame oil and seeds: this makes a superb dressing for a chicken salad.

pastes

A vast and colourful array of savoury pastes, sourced from Europe, Asia, Africa and the Americas, and based on everything from cheese to olives, nuts, fish and soya beans, can extend every discerning cook's repertoire. Furthermore, concentrated and compact as they are, pastes are perfect candidates for the storecupboard.

Be sure to look for the authentic, ethnic pastes: Italian versions of typically Mediterranean pastes, such as tomato concentrate, sun-dried tomato paste and red pesto, are usually the best.

1 Tahini This nutritious paste, popular in Middle Eastern cooking, is made from unroasted or roasted sesame seeds ground to a dense, rich sludge. Small amounts added to sauces, dips and dressings give a nutty taste, richness and gloss. It is a vital ingredient in hummus, and tastes gorgeous in North African-style lamb, with olives, lemon and pine nuts. Stand the jar in boiling water to soften the mixture, and then mix thoroughly before use.

2 Peanut butter Either crunchy or smooth, this paste of roasted peanuts (groundnuts) is humble but convenient and very nutritious, consisting of 30 per cent protein. Infinitely adaptable in cooking, it can thicken a sauce, and is a great short-cut, for making gado gado sauce, for example. Mixed with soy sauce, spices, lime juice, chilli and stock, it makes a quick hot sauce for fish, poultry, vegetables, noodles or rice.

3 Tomato paste Sometimes called tomato concentrate, this paste is made from sun- or kiln-dried tomatoes, flavoured with minimal spices, herbs and seasonings. A tablespoon is all you need to flavour and colour a dish, the double-concentrated paste being the most effective.

4 Sun-dried tomato paste This is a relatively recent arrival in the supermarkets. You may need to hunt around for a good one: look for one with 65 per cent or more tomato solids, and flavourings such as chillies, oregano and garlic. It is useful mainly in Mediterranean-style dishes, but try it also in Asian chicken and fish dishes, when a fruit-sweet taste is needed.

5 Red pesto (pesto rosso) Unlike green pesto, red pesto survives processing well. Made of tomato concentrate, olive oil, pecorino or grana cheeses, basil, garlic and pine nuts, it is superb stirred into hot pasta or into rich meat casseroles. Try it, also, on bruschetta with a drizzle of olive oil.

6 Patum Peperium Nicknamed 'Gentlemen's Relish', this salty, anchovy-based paste became a favourite British condiment in the 19th century. It looks unalluring but is surprisingly tasty. Try it on toasted muffins, or under grilled cheese on toast; or use it to make anchovy and lemon butter for steaks or baked fish.

7 Olive paste Thick, salty and earthy Mediterranean olive pastes are made from either green (unripe, sharp) or black (ripe, fruitier) olives, with flavourings such as garlic and herbs added. Use them on pizzas or in pasta, or with crudités. Tapenade is similar, but contains capers, tuna and anchovies, and is best made fresh.

8 Green pesto (pesto Genovese) This sharply pungent, fresh basil-scented paste, a speciality of Genoa, is essential for such Mediterranean dishes as minestrone, soups and pastas, and is also excellent with fish. It should contain fresh basil, garlic, pine nuts, Parmesan or pecorino cheese, and olive oil. Avoid heat-treated versions of pesto.

9 Shrimp paste A sticky paste made from fermented shrimp underpins many Southeast Asian dishes. It must always be cooked before use. With an intensely salty tang, a little shrimp paste goes a long way. Use it in sauces, soups, braising liquids, stews, stir-fries and curries. Bean curd, soy beans, and other mild-tasting proteins benefit from its use.

10 Miso Made of fermented soya beans and cereal grains, this salty paste is vital in Japanese cooking. It is the mainstay of Japanese soups, poaching stocks and pouring sauces, and is popular in Southeast Asia and China, too.

Many types of miso are available, varying in colour, texture, fragrance and sweetness. The most common type, rice miso, is called *komemiso* and comes in different colours: the deeper the colour the more mature and salty the paste. 'Red' miso (deep red to dark brown) is strong and salty, while 'white' miso (yellow to brown) has a lighter flavour.

Heat miso gently, and never boil it. Use it like a stock base, in a condiment sauce, in soup, or to add richness. It is superb combined with garlic, ginger, chilli or citrus tastes.

11 Chinese bean pastes These salty-sweet Chinese condiments, made from fermented soya beans, are similar to Japanese miso, but tend to be coarser. They can be either smooth or with some whole or fragmented beans in it (in which case the pastes may be labelled 'crushed').

Yellow bean paste (a) is milder and sweeter than dark bean sauces. Use it in stir-fries, curries, vegetable dishes, pickles, stews, braised dishes and with seafood soups. Thick black bean paste (b), popular in Malaysia and Southeast Asia, can be used in similar ways to yellow bean paste, and is also useful as a condiment in its own right.

hot sauces, pastes and condiments

All around the globe, hot sauces and pastes are used to add colour, flavour and interest to mild-flavoured foods, whether they are used as a cooking ingredient or as a table condiment. Many of the items featured on this page have a long shelf life, and need no refrigeration.

1 Smoky barbecue sauce At its best, this is a sweet, sharp, richly fruity and spicy sauce, with an appealing smoky taste. Use it on grilled or barbecued foods, or in burgers. Diluted with water or wine, it can become a stewing medium. Beaten into butter, with mustard, it makes a good glaze.

2 Worcestershire sauce Lea & Perrin's famous sauce – thin and spicy with a fruity heat and mild acidity – is, to British people, what soy sauce is to Asians. Use it shaken over grilled foods, sausages and roasted meats; or in cheesy foods such as Welsh rarebit. In stir-fries, stews and sauces, it adds character and cuts sweetness.

3 Chilli sauce Innumerable types of chilli sauce exist, made in all parts of the globe. Some are thin, others are dense; some are chunky, others are puréed. Always look for authentic products and pair them up with food that relates to that culture. Hugely versatile, chilli sauce can be used in any way imaginable,

whether added early on in cooking, later on for real heat, or as a table condiment.

4 Sweet chilli sauce Sometimes called 'dim sum dipping sauce', this translucent, fiery, sweet and garlicky sauce has many variations. Perfect with Hong Kong Chinese dishes, or Vietnamese and Thai foods, its stickiness makes it good in glazes and sauces. With soy sauce and citrus juice, it makes the perfect dipping sauce.

5 Chilli jam This dense and sticky condiment, made of red chillies, sugar, acid of some kind and usually garlic, is superb with Asian, Middle Eastern and North African dishes. It works well with curries, birianis, dhals and rice, and tastes superb with all kinds of Indian breads. A little goes a long way.

6 Tabasco sauce This classic super-hot sauce from Louisiana, instantly recognisable in its trademark bottle, contains only chillies, vinegar and salt. The classic red Tabasco sauce

(a), is made of pequin chillies, while green Tabasco (b) is made of jalapeño chillies.

Splendid either as table condiment or to cook with, Tabasco gives a lift to an amazing assortment of foods, including oysters, guacamole, blue cheese sauce and egg-fried rice.

7 Sambal oelek The Indonesian/Malaysian word 'sambal' covers a wide range of hot or spicy side dishes and condiments. *Sambal oelek*, the basic sambal, consists of chillies crushed up with salt and lemon juice. The most authentic versions are Indonesian.

Spicy, fruity, chewy and intense, sambal oelek excels as a relish – serve it with satay, for example – and also as an ingredient: it peps up everything from curries and stir-fries to chutneys and pickles.

8 Horseradish sauce A good-quality horseradish sauce is great with roast beef and smoked fish, particularly salmon, eel, trout and mackerel, as well as in some butters and dressings.

1   2   3   4

5   6a   6b   7   8

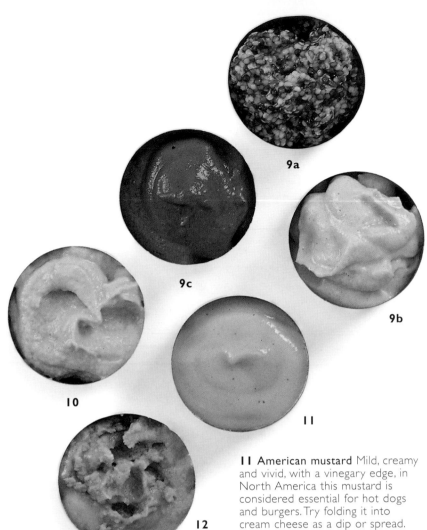

9a

9c

9b

10

11

12

13 Caribbean jerk paste Smooth, spicy and fiery, Caribbean jerk paste is fruity but also acidic. Use it in a marinade, or for grilling, baking or barbecuing; or add it to beans and rice. Mixed with coconut milk, it suits quickly cooked fish and seafood dishes.

14 Curry paste Although authentic curries often need to start from dry spices, even Indian cooks use ready-made curry pastes. These can be rubbed on foods before cooking, or added later on.

There are vast numbers of these pastes on the market. Kashmiri curry paste (a) and Bombay masala, for example, are Indian pastes, while Nonya and Laksa are South-east Asian. Thai curry pastes, including massaman, Thai red and Thai green (b), are particularly useful and usually excellent. If you have rice, canned coconut milk, and some chicken, fish or vegetables, a Thai curry is only 20 minutes away.

15 Harissa paste This delectable, fiery, fruity but sharp purée of chilli, garlic and spices is a staple of North African cuisines. Tunisian-made versions are the best. Harissa is essential with couscous and many tagines, and boosts chicken and lamb stews, and vegetable and rice dishes. It can even improve pasta and dressings.

11 American mustard Mild, creamy and vivid, with a vinegary edge, in North America this mustard is considered essential for hot dogs and burgers. Try folding it into cream cheese as a dip or spread.

12 Wasabi This fiery, aromatic paste is the essential condiment for Japanese sashimi and sushi. It is available as a paste or as a dry powder. Real wasabi, made from a horseradish-like plant, is expensive. Cheap copies are often a horseradish-mustard mix. Use it in mayonnaise, vinaigrettes, in broths and fish stews. It is also excellent with oily fish and rare-cooked beef.

9 French mustard Meaux mustard, or coarse-grain mustard (a), is superbly textural and only mildly hot. It is often used to accompany roasted meats. The most popular French mustard, however, is Dijon mustard (b). Sharp, hot and clean-tasting, this is the mustard to eat with grilled meats, especially pork, and to use in French or other creamy sauces, and in vinaigrettes. Folded into crème fraîche, Dijon mustard is superb with smoked mackerel. Bordeaux mustard (c), sometimes known simply as 'French mustard', is fruity-hot and pleasantly spicy. Milder and more earthy than Dijon, it is best used straight, with pork pies, gammon, sausages and cured meats.

10 English mustard Hotter than the French equivalent, English mustard is an essential accompaniment to British classics such as roast beef and gammon. It excels in gravies, sauces and dressings, and in cooked cheese dishes such as soufflés. Try it mixed, half and half, with apricot jam as a hot, fruity glaze for roast meats.

13

14b

14a

15

kebabs with satay sauce

Serves 4 as a starter

Slice 400g lean, boneless chicken into about 30 thin strips. Push these, concertina-style, on to 12 soaked satay sticks. Grind 2 teaspoons each of pan-toasted cumin and coriander seeds, ground turmeric and desiccated coconut, to a powder. In a pan, combine these spices with 2 tablespoons each of fish sauce, sambal oelek, palm sugar and peanut butter, adding 50ml canned coconut milk. Simmer for 5 minutes. Cool. Stir in another 150ml coconut milk. Use half to marinate the 12 chicken skewers for 20 minutes. Drain. Grill the kebabs for 2–3 minutes each side, until cooked through. Serve with the reserved satay sauce, fresh coriander and lime halves.

spare ribs with barbecue sauce

Serves 4 as a starter

Oven-poach 750g pork spare ribs with 600ml boiling water, 1 cinnamon stick and 2 tablespoons malt vinegar in an oven preheated to 150°C/Gas 2 for about 50 minutes. In a pan, combine 100ml tomato ketchup with 30ml each of Worcestershire, black bean, sweet chilli, horseradish and soy sauces. Whisk in 1 teaspoon each of Chinese five-spice powder and Cajun spice mix, adding 2 teaspoons toasted sesame oil. Coat the ribs with the mixture and set them on oiled foil. Bake in an oven preheated to 180°C/Gas 4 for 25–35 minutes or until tender and glazed.

duck breast salad with fruity sauce

Serves 4

Season and cook 4 Barbary duck breasts on a pre-heated griddle for 2–3 minutes on each side, until golden outside and rosy inside. Let them rest for a few minutes, then slice. Set on cooked rice noodles, and add baby salad leaves. For the sauce, combine 2 tablespoons each of hoisin, plum, sweet chilli and light soy sauces. Add 2 teaspoons dark sesame oil, 1 teaspoon garlic purée and a squeeze of fresh orange juice. Serve spooned over the duck slices.

prawns with spicy mayonnaise

Serves 4

Set 3 cooked jumbo prawn tails (shelled) on each of 4 serving dishes, with a dish for the mayonnaise alongside. Grind a large pinch of saffron threads with 1/2 teaspoon sea salt and 1/4 teaspoon cayenne using a pestle and mortar. Add 2 teaspoons Pernod or Aquavit, and stir in 2 teaspoons each of harissa, Dijon mustard and anchovy sauce. Stir this into 120ml mayonnaise until barely blended. Divide among the 4 serving dishes, ready for the prawn tails to be dipped in.

mustard chicken with colcannon

This recipe uses two mustards: a grainy type as the coating for the chicken and smooth Dijon mustard in the sauce, which helps to flavour and thicken it, and also gives colour and body.

Serves 4

Ingredients
4 corn-fed, free-range chicken
  breasts, boned
1 tbsp cornflour, arrowroot or rice
  flour
4 tbsp grainy mustard, such as
  Meaux or coarse-grain honey
  mustard
2 tbsp extra virgin olive oil
6 tbsp Dijon mustard
100ml dry white wine
salt and freshly ground black
  pepper
50ml soured cream
colcannon (to serve)

Method
1. Dust the chicken breasts all over with the cornflour, shaking off any excess. Then coat them thoroughly with the grainy mustard, using a palette knife or rubber scraper.
2. Heat the oil in a large, non-stick frying pan. Sauté the breasts for 2 minutes on each side. Turn them so the skin-side is up.
3. Stir in the Dijon mustard and the wine, and season with salt and pepper. Then cover and cook over a medium heat for 8–10 minutes longer until the sauce reduces and thickens.
4. Stir in the soured cream, shaking, not stirring, the pan.
5. Cook until the chicken is firm and the sauce creamy, 2–3 minutes, adding extra water if needed.
6. Serve the chicken on colcannon (creamy mashed potatoes with sautéed spring onions and cabbage), with the sauce poured over.

alcohols for savoury flavourings

The appropriate alcohol can transform a dish from reasonable to knock-out, and may even be essential to the dish. What would boeuf bourguignon be without a robust red wine? Some alcohols can 'cook' protein by their intensity; some add a herby, fragrant appeal to stocks and sauces; others, when reduced, can create a wonderfully rich sauce or glaze. There are few rules to follow when cooking with alcohol, except always choose a bottle that is fit enough to drink.

1   2   3   4   5   6   7   8

1 White wine Characterful, medium-dry, full-bodied white wines perform best in cooking. Sauvignons blancs and floral Gewürtztraminers and Rieslings are particularly useful. Aligoté wines are crisply dry but are superb in many fish and white-meat dishes, while oaky Chardonnay must be treated with caution since it can take over the dish. Honeyed Sauternes is superb added late in cooking.

2 Red wine Youngish, full-flavoured red wines are best for cooking, and generally need reducing by half. Beaujolais, Rioja and Grenache are all good with red meats. Pinot Noir, with a raspberry taste, plummy Merlot and peppery Shiraz are all great to cook with, too. A leg of lamb poached in Pinot Noir, which is then reduced with garlic, shallots and herbs, is fantastic.

3 Vermouth A fortified, wine-based apéritif, with a distinctive, herby aroma, vermouth marries well with foods. It can be used instead of wine, and has the advantage of lasting longer.
   White, dry vermouth (often French) works best. Try it in soups, stocks, dressings and marinades,

to deglaze a roasting pan, or for poaching fish. Use red, sweet vermouth (often Italian) in red meat glazes and pasta sauces.

4 Sherry True sherry, a fortified wine, comes from Andalusia, in Spain, and can vary hugely in colour and sweetness. The best sherries for savoury cooking are dry and pale, such as fino or manzanilla. These sherries can transform a kidney or liver dish, and work wonders in pan gravies and in sautés of pork, veal or chicken. Sherry deteriorates fast, so keep it in the fridge and use it as quickly as possible.

5 Bison grass vodka Clean and potent, vodka is usually distilled from grains. Flavours have been added for generations, and bison grass gives a particularly elegant taste, with a scent of vanilla. It is superb in dishes made with smoked oily fish (such as herring, salmon, sea trout or sturgeon).

6 Scotch whisky Whisky is made worldwide, but the best is still Scottish. For cooking, use a good blend (of malt and grain whiskies) rather than your best single malt. Whisky is excellent in game and

some beef dishes. Deglaze a roasting pan with whisky and stock or wine, swirl in some butter and then season with black pepper: simple but delicious.

7 Schnapps This is a general term that describes a range of strong northern European spirits, which are usually colourless, distilled from potatoes or grains, and flavoured with spices and citrus. Scandinavian aquavit, or akvavit, is among the best known. Use it in warm herring salad, flambéed with crayfish, or in gravadlax.

8 Rice wine This is a very popular kitchen ingredient in China and Japan. To marinate fish, season sushi and dress chicken and vegetables, these are the alcohols to choose. Chinese *shaohsing*, made from fermented glutinous rice, is added late in cooking and gives elegant, yeasty depths to drunken chicken, stir-fried duck and some soups. Japanese sake is flowery, clean-scented and delicately pale.
   Rice wines have a vaguely sherry-like flavour, and dry sherry (fino) is often substituted. Mirin, essentially a sweetened sake, is used only in cooking, often mixed with soy sauce.

stocks and stock bases

Ready-made stocks or bouillons are storecupboard basics that can save hours of time. A vast array of stocks is now available, with new types and flavours arriving on the market constantly. They all serve a similar purpose – to enrich sauces, gravies, soups, stews, stir-fries and rice dishes – but the form can dictate how you use them, and the effect can vary. Liquid stock, for example, produces a better glaze than a stock cube does. Inevitably, the less-processed products, such as jellied stock, have the better flavour, but also a shorter shelf life. Choose those with as few additives as possible. Shop-bought stocks are often salty, so don't salt food until the end of the cooking time.

1 Concentrate Strong and sweet-salty, good-quality concentrated liquid stocks are positively tasty. They can be added directly into boiling liquid, or used neat in tiny amounts: try adding a dash to risottos or mushroom recipes. A good beef concentrate could even help create a steak sauce: simply add butter and wine.

2 Fresh stock Good fresh stock should be semi-jellied, flavourful and true to its main ingredient. Fresh fish stock, boiled down with some good white wine and butter, can become a delicious sauce. Unopened, a tub of fresh stock should last for up to a week.

3 Jelly Jellied stock is perfect for spooning straight into food. Look for *glace de viande* (a), a gelatinised, reduced meat stock (usually beef or veal), which can be delicious. As much a glaze as a stock, it can be brushed over a roast to go in the oven. Added to vegetable cooking water with a knob of butter, it can make an instant gravy.

Some jellied stocks come as a paste-like concentrate (b), which can give an intense meaty richness to quickly cooked meat dishes.

4 Powder and granules Stock powders and granules dissolve quickly and can be added directly to boiling water to create a stock, or sprinkled straight into the cooking pot. Japanese dashi soup stock (a) can be used in miso soup and other speedy Asian seafood dishes, while a good vegetable bouillon powder (b) adds extra flavour to rice, grain and vegetable dishes.

5 Consommé Shop-bought consommés, often sold in cans, are useful because the equivalent meat broth takes ages to create at home. Good-quality consommés work well in French onion soup, or as part of a game stew.

6 Cubes Best crumbled into a boiling liquid to be used as a cooking medium, or sprinkled dry into stuffings or toppings, stock cubes are generally useful rather than outstanding. But there are some exceptions. Tom yam stock cubes, for example, are intensely salty, citrussy and chilli-hot, and helpful in many Southeast Asian dishes; and shiitake stock cubes give a fresh mushroomy background taste and are superb in stir-fries and rice or noodle dishes.

balsamic sabayon with salmon sashimi
Serves 4

In a small saucepan, boil 4 tablespoons Marsala and 2 tablespoons balsamic vinegar until reduced to barely 2 tablespoons, then let cool. In a small bowl over simmering water, whisk 2 egg yolks, 3 tablespoons caster sugar and 4 shakes distilled vinegar to a froth using an electric whisk. Trickle in most of the Marsala reduction, whisking for 2 minutes more. Spoon the frothy sabayon over each of 4 servings of 50g cubed, raw, sashimi-grade salmon. Add dots of the remaining Marsala reduction and red onion slices and serve.

red wine-glazed chicken breasts
Serves 4

Over a medium heat, boil 100ml robust red wine with 15g *glace de viande*, 1 tablespoon raspberry vinegar, 2 tablespoons raspberry jelly and 25g salted butter until reduced to a sticky glaze. Sauté 4 chicken breasts in oil or butter and add them to the glaze, turning to coat. Slice the chicken breasts and spoon the glaze over, then scatter over a teaspoon of pink peppercorns, if liked, and add a pile of baby leaf salad.

jellied beef consommé with sherry
Serves 4

Freeze 1 unopened 400ml can good-quality beef consommé for 3–4 hours until semi-jellied. Finely dice a 7.5cm chunk peeled cucumber, and divide among 4 soup cups. Whisk 4 tablespoons fino sherry into the consommé, using a fork. Pour this into the cups and top with 1 tablespoon soured cream, 1 teaspoon trout or salmon roe, and dill sprigs. Serve immediately.

vodka shooters with oysters
Serves 4

In a cocktail shaker, with ice, shake together 300ml tomato juice, the juice of 1 lemon, and 4 shakes each of Tabasco, Worcestershire and tamarind sauces. Add ½ teaspoon each of horseradish sauce, celery salt, Cajun spice mix and sherry vinegar. Shake again and pour into 4 iced shot glasses. Carefully, over a teaspoon, pour 2 tablespoons ice-cold vodka into each and garnish with celery. Set 1 raw, live oyster next to each glass. Gulp the oyster then sip the vodka shooter.

sweet flavourings

1   2a   2b

3   4   5

sugar

Sugar, prized for its sweetness, is a symbol of ripeness. It can be produced from all sorts of trees and plants, often in the form of syrups (see pages 42–3), but crystal sugar is its most useful form. The greatest variety of sugars come from sugar cane, produced by varying degrees of refining. The cruder, less refined states taste most distinctive, while highly refined white sugar tastes just sweet. (Most refined white sugar comes from sugar beet and is chemically identical to refined cane sugar.)

1 Caster sugar With its fine grains, caster sugar incorporates more air than other sugars, which makes it perfect for creating lightness in cake mixtures, crisp biscuits and frothy desserts. It is good in clear syrups and glazes, and can be ground up with spices such as cinnamon, cloves and coriander as a sweet, spicy sprinkle.

Caster sugar is used to make vanilla sugar, the best versions of which are flavoured with real vanilla seeds. This is excellent sprinkled over raw fruits and yoghurts, it scents syrups and cakes beautifully, and it can improve biscuits, glazes and chocolate desserts.

2 Granulated sugar This medium-grained, free-flowing sugar is the workhorse of the kitchen and comes either as golden (a) or white (b). It is the most valuable type of sugar for everyday use and the most versatile. It can be used in both raw and cooked dishes, including cakes.

3 Sugar lumps Made of granulated sugar moulded into shapes, then oven-dried, sugar lumps (which may be neatly square or more roughly shaped) are good in situations where ingredients need to be crushed – with mint leaves for mint sauce, for example – or as part of a sugar-spice sprinkle for an apple pie topping.

4 Jam sugar The coarse crystals of jam sugar contain added pectin and citric acid, which help to set jams and jellies. The crystals dissolve slowly and evenly, avoiding the risks of caramelising or burning on the base of the pan. Often, less boiling time is required, which helps to preserve the fruit flavours.

5 Icing sugar Powdery, sweet and brilliant white, icing sugar gives a fairytale prettiness to cakes, biscuits, soft fruits and pastries when sprinkled on using a sieve. It dissolves instantly, so it is also useful for uncooked mixtures, such as icings, glazes, marzipans and chocolate truffles. Royal icing sugar has powdered egg white added, which helps pliability, for decorating cakes.

understanding the label

Due to the liberal use of words such as 'unrefined' and 'raw', it can be hard to decipher the labelling on many sugars. In reality, virtually all sugars are refined to some degree, but the less refined sugars retain more natural molasses than their bleached white counterparts. The former include the big-selling golden caster and granulated sugars, at one end of the spectrum, and the brown sugars at the other. Many commercial brown sugars, particularly those labelled as 'soft light brown' or 'soft dark brown', however, are made by coating refined sugar with caramel or molasses. The list of ingredients should make clear whether you are dealing with the real thing. Genuine brown sugars, such as muscovado and molasses sugar, are less widely available but far superior.

6 Muscovado sugar Relatively unrefined and rich in natural molasses, muscovado sugar is dark, moist and intensely fragrant. It is either light or dark, depending on the molasses content, and has oodles more flavour than ordinary soft brown sugar. It works well in sprinkled toppings, gingerbread and fruit cakes (it gives good-keeping quality to cakes), in pickles and in fresh Asian relishes.

Barbados sugar, which is similar, has a butterscotch sweetness and is good in chocolate and Christmas cakes, and in Caribbean dishes.

7 Demerara Named after the area in British Guyana where it was first produced, demerara sugar is mellow-flavoured but hard and crunchy. Use it when a gritty, grainy texture is wanted: to top a muffin, or in a sprinkled crumb topping, for example. It is good in gingerbread and also in savoury dishes: use some pounded together with sea salt, lemon zest and lime leaves to rub over fish before baking or barbecuing. (Always check the label when buying demerara sugar; avoid those that are produced artificially, by coating regular sugar with caramel or molasses.)

8 Molasses sugar A minimally refined, raw sugar, molasses sugar is fine, dark and crumbly and has a treacly, rich, spicy flavour. Use it as you would muscovado, but also in spicy syrups, glazes, savoury preserves, or savoury-sweet spice mixes. It goes well with citrus flavours, cocoa and chocolate.

9 Palm sugar This crude, dense sugar, made from crystallised palm sap, can come from a variety of different palms and is used in much savoury cooking in Asia, Latin America and the Caribbean. It is often found in Indian shops, under the name jaggery. Palm sugar has an aromatic, fudgy-sweet freshness and works well in recipes with coconut, chillies, lemongrass, ginger, garlic, fish sauce and spices.

10 Rock crystal sugar These hard, golden and shiny crystals (also known as rock sugar, or yellow lump sugar), are considered by many Chinese cooks to be sugar in its most desirable form. Ground to a gritty powder, or dissolved in hot liquid, rock crystal sugar can be used in desserts, glazes, or for sweetening stews or sweetmeats.

11 Dehydrated sugar cane juice A soft, intense, fudge-like sugar, this part-refined sugar suits Caribbean, Asian and Southeast Asian recipes. In savoury and sweet dishes, it adds density, colour and viscosity, whether used straight or crushed, grated, chopped or crumbled, in a syrup or as part of a sauce.

12 Sugar swizzle sticks These decorative sugar-tipped stirring sticks are often used to sweeten coffee or tea. Made from glassy, crystal sugar, which is intensely sweet and slow to dissolve, they can be used to crush fresh rosemary, verbena or other herbs into boiling water for a refreshing hot drink.

storage

Moist brown sugars, such as muscovado, clump and go hard if exposed to dry air. Store them airtight, and resoften by covering the sugar, in a bowl, with a damp cloth. Caster sugar that has caked hard can be simply crushed using a rolling pin.

syrups

Essential in the kitchen for adding sweetness, gloss and texture to both sweet and savoury dishes, syrups have many different sources. Some syrups occur naturally, such as honeycomb, while others are made by gathering, boiling and concentrating the sap from plants and trees, such as bamboo or palm trees, or by heat-treating starches, such as maize. Most significant, however, are the syrups made from sugar cane – the crude residues from the sugar-boiling process that are known, generically, as treacle. Even golden syrup, the most refined of these, contains 'impurities', which are what give these syrups colour and taste.

There are also many fruit syrups, honeys and flower-scented syrups on the market, which can be fun to experiment with. They include pomegranate and other fruit syrups, popular in the Middle East, which are made by boiling down fruit to create sweet-sour molasses. And don't neglect the syrups that come with canned or bottled fruits (see page 62), which are often well worth using.

I Honeycomb This fascinating product is honey in its own natural package of beeswax cells. It is delicious crushed on hot buttered sourdough toast, or crush it over Greek yoghurt or soft ricotta cheese for a quick dessert (discarding the wax after chewing if you prefer, though the wax is harmless).

2 Corn syrup Available either light (pictured) or rich dark brown (with molasses added), this heavy syrup is made from maize starch; similar versions are now also made from wheat starch.

Extremely sweet, and sometimes vanilla-scented, it is useful for keeping creamed mixtures emulsified and stable. It keeps butter icings creamy, and is useful in some toffees, ice creams, icings and rich, damp cake mixtures. It is invaluable in pecan pie, and useful, too, in mixtures used as glazes for roasts.

3 Pomegranate molasses When fresh pomegranate juice is reduced down to a thick, dark syrup, it is beautifully sweet-sour, and useful for both seasoning and in sweet and savoury cooking. Popular above all in Iran, it is also used in other Middle Eastern cuisines, but has arrived only relatively recently in Western supermarkets.

Chicken, pheasant or duck cooked in pomegranate molasses,

with walnuts, is a famous Iranian dish known as *faisinjan*. You can also use the syrup to deglaze the pan when cooking steaks or sausages, or to rub over roasted joints. Use it in glazes, or diluted as cooking stock for pork or game.

Don't confuse pomegranate molasses with sweet pomegranate syrup, which is pink and sickly.

4 Malt extract This dense, syrupy extract, made from malted grain, is used mainly in beer- and whisky-making, but it is a pity not to use it in home cooking. It can part-replace golden syrup, maple syrup or molasses to create a more subtle taste. Try it in wholewheat loaves, flapjacks or baked and steamed puddings. It is also lovely spooned over thick cream, yoghurt, fromage frais or porridge.

5 Blackstrap molasses The crudest form of molasses, from which virtually all the sugar has been extracted, blackstrap molasses has an almost acrid bitterness but a perceptible sweetness as well; it is also high in minerals. Use molasses to enrich and darken biscuits, fruit cakes and steamed puddings.

6 Black treacle A sweeter version of blackstrap molasses, black treacle still has a sharp, almost bitter, accent and a tarry depth of flavour. It is useful in dark, dense, baked mixtures, such as gingerbread, and can also add depth and complexity to plum pudding, treacle toffees and fruit cakes.

7 Maple syrup The boiled-down sap of certain kinds of maple tree native to Canada and the United States, maple syrup is wonderful poured neat over pancakes and blini, and it makes a delicious sweetener for cakes, biscuits, fruit puddings and ice cream. Or try mixing it with mustard and vinegar as a glaze for ham or carrots.

Beware of the 'maple-flavoured' counterfeits – a maple leaf on the label guarantees authenticity.

8 Honey This age-old food, made by bees from flower nectar, is sweeter than sugar. Single-flower honeys are generally the best (and most expensive), but cheaper honeys from mixed flowers can be good, especially if flavoured with wild flowers. As a general rule, the darker the colour of the honey, the stronger the flavour.

Set honey (a) is produced either naturally, through crystallisation, or artificially, through heating. Naturally set white clover honey from New Zealand is intensely flavourful and excellent for general use. Mix it with butter, orange juice and zest and bitter chocolate as a frosting for cakes, or combine it with cream and cinnamon as a sauce for ice cream or baked fruits. A good, aromatic clear honey (b), such as lavender honey from Provence, is very floral and tastes delicious drizzled over cream-topped fruits, and it can also be used as a glaze.

9 Fruit syrup The best fruit syrups are intense and scented, and contain a high percentage of fruit and little else; the best versions are often Belgian, Swiss, Dutch, French or German. They come in different flavours, such as peach-passion fruit (pictured), red fruits, or apple and pear, and can be useful in fruit tarts, pies, compotes, fruit salads and ice cream, matched with similar fruits; drizzle them over cheesecakes or panna cotta.

10 Crème de cassis This intensely sweet but sharp blackcurrant liqueur is totally luscious when folded through thick cream, yoghurt, fromage frais or custard, or drizzled over lemon chocolate or bitter chocolate mousse. In red wine jelly, with berry fruits, it is absolutely glorious.

11 Elderflower cordial The best elderflower cordial, flowery and Muscat-scented, is made by steeping elderflower blossoms in liquid with sugar, lemon and citric acid. It is both sweet and sharp. Use the cordial, diluted, as a drink, or add some to weak black tea instead of lemon. Or try pouring some over fritters or over melon, and use it to dampen cakes in trifle-style desserts, or to sweeten apple puddings.

12 Golden syrup A unique British creation, golden syrup is a more refined product than black treacle. Densely thick, clear and sweet, it is scrumptious spread on muffins or scones, or poured over suet puddings. It adds an interesting sweetness and moistness to cakes and steamed puddings, and is essential in treacle tart. With butter and cream, it makes fudge sauce. Or mix it with vinegar and spices to brush over meats as a glaze.

13 Caramello liquido This sticky, caramelised sugar syrup gives instant richness, colour and flavour. The best versions are made in Spain or Latin America. Try it trickled into marinades, glazes and sauces, or whisk it into or drizzle it over yoghurt or ricotta for a quick dessert. It suits cinnamon, cloves, dark rum, dried fruits, citrus and creamy mixtures. Brushed over meat to be roasted, liquid caramel adds curious charm and gloss.

scented stock syrup

Makes 850ml

This classic syrup has many uses: as a pastry glaze, to sweeten sour fruit juices, or to pour over sliced fresh fruits. Kept in a cool, dark place, it lasts for months. Combine 500g caster or granulated sugar, 2 tablespoons liquid glucose syrup, 2 tablespoons lemon juice and 500ml boiling water in a saucepan. Heat, stirring, until it comes to the boil, then simmer for 5 minutes or until clear. Remove from the heat and cool slightly over iced water. While still warm, add a 15cm strip lemon zest, and a cinnamon stick or vanilla pod, if liked. When quite cold, add 3 tablespoons white rum or schnapps. Pour into a bottle and shake.

caramelised nuts for praline

Pounded to a powder, or praline, caramelised nuts add great colour, taste and texture to ice-cream, yoghurt, creamy custards or plain pastries. First, put 75g blanched almonds or mixed nuts on to a flexible metal tray. Measure 100g granulated sugar into a clean, dry frying pan. Place over a high heat and shake the pan horizontally, never stirring (to prevent the formation of crystals), and continue to cook; the base layer will melt first, followed by the upper layer. Turn down the heat to medium-low, and continue to cook, using the same movements, until the caramel turns from pale to medium gold. Carefully pour it over the nuts, and leave for 3–5 minutes to set and cool. Twist the metal tray and splinter off chunks of nut brittle. Pound these to a coarse or fine powder, and store in an airtight container.

steamed ginger puddings

These soft and steamy individual puddings have the unexpected bite of stem ginger in syrup, and golden syrup to sweeten them. Serve with custard or cream.

Serves 4

Ingredients
125g salted soft-spread butter
125g caster sugar
2 eggs, beaten
125g self-raising flour, sifted
1 tsp baking powder, sifted
4 tbsp scented stock syrup
  (see opposite) or golden syrup
  (melted)

For the topping:
4 stem ginger chunks, finely sliced
4 tsp stem ginger syrup
4 tsp golden syrup, maple syrup or
  clear honey

Method
1. Have ready a large steamer. Butter four 175ml heatproof bowls (non-metal if using a microwave).
2. Cream the butter, sugar, eggs and 2 tablespoons of the flour together in a medium-sized bowl, using an electric whisk or rotary beater. Add the remaining flour and the baking powder, and gently stir in the scented stock syrup (or golden syrup).
3. Divide the pudding mixture between the prepared bowls. Place these in the steamer and cover all four with one large sheet of oiled aluminium foil. Steam for 25–30 minutes, until firm and risen: a metal skewer, inserted into one of the puddings, should come out clean. (Alternatively, microwave on High for 6–8 minutes.)
4. Turn the puddings out on 4 serving plates. Pile slices of ginger on top of each, and drizzle with some of both syrups. Serve with vanilla custard or cream, if liked.

essences and flavoured waters

In everyday life, we are often unaware of the significance of aromatics, but a sip of an almond-scented cappuccino or a bite of an orange flower-scented madeleine rarely fails to trigger feelings of comfort and well-being. When using these volatile flavours, however, we must be discreet. Most essences and flavoured waters are highly concentrated and should be used in tiny amounts: add them drop by drop, particularly if using strong flavours such as bitter almond. Essences should usually be added late in the cooking process.

I Bitter almond essence Made from roasted bitter almonds, the essence of which is dissolved out in oil, this concentrated flavouring has a bitter-sweet and lingering taste. It works well with fruits of the apricot and cherry family, and is the crucial flavour in marzipan, macaroons and frangipane. Note that plain almond essence is not the same thing.

2 Peppermint oil Clear, intense, and almost medicinal in taste, this flavouring creates a coolness that offsets the sweet, rich taste of chocolate, for example. A few drops can improve fresh fruit salads.

3 Vanilla extract Vanilla pods, macerated in alcohol, create a densely aromatic extract, or essence; beware of those that contain synthetic 'vanillin' flavour. Use vanilla extract towards the end of cooking, in ice cream, custards, milky sauces and puddings.

4 Rose water (rose flower water) Steam-distilled from rose petals, rose water is floral and intensely musky. Double- or triple-distilled types are the best buy. Perhaps best known for its use in Turkish delight, rose water also goes well with berries: try raspberry and rose ice cream, for example.

5 Orange flower water This citrus-sweet liquid, also known as orange blossom water, is distilled from the white blossoms of bitter oranges. Superb in fruit or rice desserts, it also excels in combination with dates, nuts, honey and yoghurt or cream.

6 Tea If using tea as a flavouring, it pays to use a good-quality one. Black and green teas are the most useful. Earl Grey tea (a), a black tea, has an intense, sweet-citrussy appeal and tannic intensity. Brew it in boiling milk as the basis of tea ice cream, or use it in syrups, or to rehydrate dried fruits. Green tea, intensely floral and scented perhaps with passion fruit (b), or hand-rolled and exquisitely delicate (c), can be used as a broth for poaching duck or chicken. Chinese white tea (d) is a fascinating product only recently introduced to Europe, and comes in beautifully hand-twisted shapes. Similar to, but less tannic than, green tea, white tea can be used as a cooking liquid for delicate white meats or fish.

7 Coffee For cooking purposes, coffee is best made from high-quality roasted coffee beans (a), ground at the time of use and brewed using near-boiling water. Select a good blend such as mocha and Java, and use it, fortified, in cakes, creamy mousses, tiramisu-type desserts, or in caramel, butterscotch and toffee sauces.

Unroasted coffee beans (b) are hard to find, but provide a great flavour when freshly roasted. Put the beans in a heavy-based frying pan over medium to high heat, and shake, stir and turn them regularly; remove when browned and aromatic, and grind them once cooled.

6a

6b

6d

6c

7b

7a

alcohols for sweet flavourings

With relatively little effort, you can use characterful, good-quality alcohols to achieve fascinating complexity and outrageously delicious effects. Use them as you would essences, added little and late for background flavours. Alternatively, you can splash alcohols generously into everything from custards and compotes to jellies, cakes and preserves. Try to contrast long-aged spirits with the sweet-sharp shock of pineapple, passion fruit or raspberry. Macerate raisins in rum, make a ginger wine-enriched ganache: the possibilities are endless.

1 Bitters These spirit-based tonic mixers, flavoured with bitter herbs, roots and flowers, give a spicy, aromatic bitterness to both sweet and savoury dishes: add a few drops to ice creams or fruit salads, or to marinades and stews. Most famous is brick-red Angostura (pictured), traditionally used in pink gin.

2 Gin The herbal intensity of gin goes well with apple and cinnamon dishes, pears in cardamom-scented syrup, blackcurrant desserts, and lemon and orange ices and cheesecakes. Add gin early in cooking, flambé it to evaporate off the alcohol, or add it late to keep its full power.

3 Cognac Brandy is more useful in cooking than any other spirit, and Cognac, from France, is as good as brandy gets. It is excellent for flambéed pancakes, it enriches fruit cakes, helps to preserve jams, and excels in chocolate, vanilla, coffee and cream desserts.

4 Ginger wine This spicy wine is made from fortified raisin wine, which is steeped in ground ginger for weeks, and matured for a year. It enriches soups and can be used in glazes for pastries.

5 Cointreau This brandy-based, triple sec spirit is flavoured with bitter orange peel and aromatics. Syrupy sweet, citrussy and herbal, Cointreau is excellent in chocolate-, citrus- and even coffee-flavoured desserts. It also works well in cakes, pastries, mousses and jellies.

6 Dark rum Most commonly distilled from cane-sugar molasses, dark rums are ripe, fruity and fiery. They can be used in confectionery, syrups, sauces, butters, creams, custards and ice cream. Drizzled over warm cakes or pastries, or in fruit purées, a combination of rum and citrus zest works wonders. Potent Stroh rum, from Austria, is excellent in plum pastries and sweet sauces.

7 Port The only major fortified wine to be based on red wine, this delicious Portuguese spirit works well in sweet cheese pastries, nut desserts, jellies and dried fruit dishes, or can be used to fortify jams and compotes.

8 Marsala Available in varying degrees of strength and sweetness, this fortified wine from Sicily is rich, mellow and sticky, and perfect for many cooking tasks. It is the classic alcohol to use in zabaglione and tiramisu.

9 Sweet sherry Delicious sweet sherry from Spain is essential in English trifle. Amontillado (medium sweet) and oloroso (sweet and intensely rich) can both be drizzled over steam puddings or used in Christmas pudding or fruit cakes. Sponge fingers, soaked in sherry, and layered with hot caramel sauce, nuts and mascarpone, makes a sensational dessert.

tiramisu

This classic Italian dessert is voluptuously textured, and combines the rich, smoky flavour of fortified wine with the aromas of vanilla and coffee. It is easily achieved using almost all store-cupboard ingredients. Make it quickly just before serving or chill it for up to 8 hours beforehand.

Serves 4

Ingredients
6 tbsp freshly made hot, strong coffee
8 tbsp sweet Marsala or Madeira
2 tbsp dark rum, Cognac or amaretto
1 tsp vanilla extract
16 sponge finger biscuits
2 x 400g pots mascarpone, beaten until smooth
1 tbsp cocoa, sifted
1 tbsp icing sugar, sifted

Method
1. Pour the first four ingredients into a shallow dish, and mix together.
2. Quickly dip each sponge finger into the coffee mixture, and set aside on a piece of foil.
3. Whisk half the remaining liquid into one pot of the mascarpone.
4. Make a criss-cross using two dipped sponge fingers in the base of each of 4 serving glasses or dishes. Drizzle over some of the remaining coffee mixture and spoon in some of the flavoured mascarpone.
5. Repeat this process of layering, finishing with the plain mascarpone spooned over the top.
6. Drizzle any remaining coffee syrup over, and dust with the cocoa and icing sugar, sifted together. Serve immediately or chill.

poached fruits in lemon verbena and caramelised seeds

Raymond Blanc, the creative and innovative chef-patron of Le Manoir aux Quat' Saisons, near Oxford, devised this refreshing dish, which uses a scented herb tea to infuse delicate flavours and create a light fruit syrup for dried fruits. With some toasted nuts and seeds sprinkled on top, and perhaps a dollop of fromage frais or Greek yoghurt, it makes a delicious breakfast or dessert dish.

Serves 4

Ingredients

- 4 tbsp lemon verbena, chopped, or other herbal tea: jasmine, ginger or red fruit
- 12 Agen prunes, soaked (these have the best flavour and hold their texture when soaked)
- 2 ripe Williams or Comice pears, skin on, core removed, cut lengthways into 8 segments
- 1 heaped tbsp each of sunflower seeds, pine kernels, flaxseeds, pumpkin seeds and flaked almonds
- 1 heaped tbsp maple syrup
- 1 dried fig, flattened with the back of your hand, then finely sliced
- 1 tsp finely sliced peppermint or 4 fresh mint sprigs (optional)

Method

1. Boil 300ml of water and pour it over the chopped verbena or your tea of choice and leave to infuse for 5 minutes. Strain the warm tea over the Agen prunes and leave to soak for 8–12 hours.
2. Lift the prunes out of the tea using a slotted spoon and put them to one side. Pour the juice from the prunes into a saucepan, add the pear segments, cover with a lid, bring to the boil and simmer for 30 seconds. If the pears you are using are slightly underripe, cook them for a further 2 minutes. Remove from the heat and allow the pears to cool in the liquid.
3. To cook the seeds, preheat the oven to 220°C/Gas 7. Mix the seeds into the maple syrup and then spread over a nonstick baking tray. Roast in the oven for 8 minutes until lightly golden brown, then remove and put to one side. Toasting the seeds intensifies their flavour; you can also do this under a grill if necessary.
4. To serve, divide the caramelised seeds between 4 bowls, arrange the poached pears and prunes on top and scatter the sliced fig over the fruits. Divide the cooking juices between the bowls, and, if you want, sprinkle sliced peppermint or fresh mint sprigs on top.

spreads, pastes and conserves

The best types of sweet spreads, pastes and conserves can widen a cook's repertoire considerably. Because, in most cases, water has been evaporated off in the cooking, these foods are usually concentrated and flavourful. The nature of their manufacture also means that they have a long shelf life.

The most desirable spreads and conserves have realistic colours – which may be muted rather than brilliant – and pleasing textures: nougat, for example, should have a dense, chewy texture rather than a soft and sticky, glucose-boosted consistency; while good jams should have an appealing, soft consistency, and not be hard and sticky due to the excessive use of setting agents. The best jams are those with refreshingly few ingredients: fruit, sugar and perhaps citric, tartaric or ascorbic acid to create a perfect set.

1 Cajeta (dulce de leche) Made by boiling down milk with sugar, this rich caramel is loved in Spain, Portugal and Latin America; you may also find it labelled *manjar blanco*. Scandinavians and the French produce a similar product, known as 'milk jam'. It is superb spread on sweet pancakes or toasted brioches, or folded into yoghurt or cream cheese. Whisked with milk, it makes an instant caramel shake.

2 Povidl plum paste This concentrated plum jam paste, flavoured with dark rum, is a favourite in Viennese dishes and is well worth seeking out. It can be used as a topping or heated with juice as an intensely flavoured sauce, which is excellent with cakes, pancakes and ice creams. Use it with ground poppy seeds or apple to fill pastry tartlets.

3 Membrillo (quince paste) This sticky, intensely sweet-sharp fruit 'cheese' results from the long-cooking of quince with sugar. Superb served with blue cheeses, it can also be dissolved in sweet wine and folded through soft cheese with saffron and honey as a dessert. Dice it up and bake in pastry cases for instant fruit pies, or add it to citrus fruit salads. Guava paste is a Central American equivalent.

4 Halva This name covers a wide range of Middle Eastern, Central Asian, Turkish and Greek sweetmeats. The most common type of halva found in Europe is made of ground sesame seeds and sugar syrup or honey, flavoured with nuts, candied fruits and spices. It is delicious crushed into ice cream or used to fill dried figs, dates and peaches.

5 Pavé de fruits These concentrated, sugar-coated pastes are made by boiling down the juice of naturally sharp fruits, such as blackcurrants, with sugar. These are excellent as petit fours with slivers of Parmesan pressed on top. Finely chopped, stirred into mascarpone and drizzled with Marsala, they make a quick and elegant dessert.

6 Nougat Known as nougat in English and French, *turrón* in Spanish and *torrone* in Italian, this intensely sweet paste is made of boiled honey and/or sugar syrup mixed with egg whites, nuts, vanilla and candied fruits. Use it crumbled into ice cream or crushed on scented fresh figs or ripe peaches, or layer it into a dense cake with membrillo.

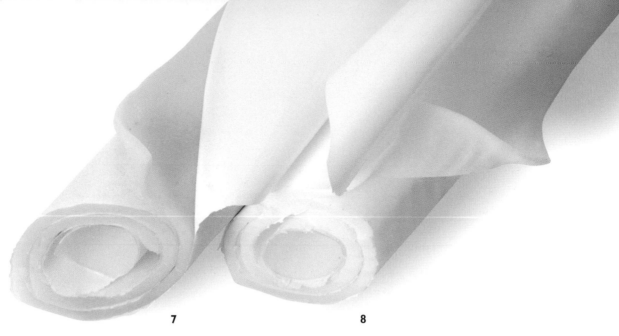

7

8

7 Marzipan This beautifully textured almond and sugar paste can be bought in convenient blocks or rolls. Startlingly yellow marzipan used to be the norm, but now more natural shades are also available. Integral to certain traditional recipes, such as stollen and simnel cake, marzipan is also used to separate a fruit cake from its royal icing (see below). It makes a good filling for pastries and chocolates, and can be coloured and layered for sweetmeats.

8 Royal icing Blocks and rolls of icing are good for speed and easy application – particularly when covering Christmas or wedding cakes. Try making it more interesting by brushing on flavourings (such as rose water or orange flower water), or by adding colour, or even gold or silver leaf.

9 Apricot jam Sharp, sweet-scented and almondy, apricot jam is an indispensable storecupboard ingredient. Melted with lemon juice and strained, it makes a superb golden glaze, for use on apple and pear tarts. Spoon it over cream cheese and serve with langues-de-chat biscuits, or fold it into whipped cream for an apricot fool.

10 Redcurrant jelly This strained fruit jelly preserve is soft but firm, sharp but fruity-sweet. It melts easily with lemon juice to form a glaze that sets on cooling: it is excellent for berry and currant

9

10

11

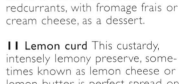

12

pastries and plum or peach tarts. Serve it melted over fresh redcurrants, with fromage frais or cream cheese, as a dessert.

11 Lemon curd This custardy, intensely lemony preserve, sometimes known as lemon cheese or lemon butter, is perfect spread on hot toast, scones or toasted muffins, but is surprisingly useful to cook with, too. It is delicious in a pavlova, covered in whipped cream or with passion fruit pulp and orange flower water folded in. Mixed with mashed bananas and yoghurt it makes a quick fruit fool. Diluted with lemon juice or white wine, it can be used as a sauce for ice cream.

12 Fruit compote Made of fruit stewed with sugar and water, compotes often go to a mush – particularly if fruits such as greengages, rhubarb or apricots are used. Other fruits, such as forest fruits or red fruits (pictured), tend to hold their shape better. When buying compotes, look for a natural colour: the fruits should retain their subtle, natural tones.

Compotes are very useful for making quick desserts. Use them in fruit pies or fools, or puréed in yoghurt drinks, or eat them straight with cream and fine crisp wafers. Or try layering the fruit with yoghurt, or setting it, using gelatine, to a jelly. Vanilla, cinnamon or citrus zest can be added to forest fruit compotes for extra flavour.

white chocolate sauce with mint

"The mint adds freshness to this sauce, which is ideal for making a marriage of two chocolate sauces with a selection of all-chocolate desserts. It is also delicious served over dark chocolate ice cream with a few pistachios scattered on top", says Michel Roux, chef-patron of the famous Waterside Inn, at Bray-on-Thames. His superb intense sauce maximises the flavours in a very effective way.

Serves 6

Ingredients
250g white couverture or
    best-quality white chocolate,
    chopped
100ml milk
250ml double cream
7g fresh mint leaves
¾ tsp caraway seeds

Method
1. Put the white chocolate in a bowl, stand it in a bain-marie and melt it gently over low heat, stirring with a wooden spoon until smooth.
2. In a saucepan, bring the milk and cream to the boil. As soon as it begins to bubble, toss in the mint leaves and caraway seeds, turn off the heat and cover the pan.
3. Leave to infuse for 10 minutes, then pass the milk through a wire-mesh conical sieve on to the melted chocolate. Mix with a whisk until thoroughly amalgamated.
4. Transfer the chocolate sauce to a clean saucepan, set over medium heat and bubble for a few seconds, whisking continuously.
5. Serve the sauce hot. If you are not serving it immediately, you can keep it warm in a bain-marie for a few minutes.

chocolate brownie cakes

These superb little soufflé-like cakes contain bitter chocolate, which trickles forth temptingly when the they are cut into. Serve either plain or with ice-cold crème fraîche.

Serves 4

Ingredients
65g salted butter, cubed
125g bitter chocolate, ideally with cocoa solids of at least 60%, broken in pieces
2 medium eggs, at room temperature
2 medium egg yolks, at room temperature
50g vanilla sugar
4 tsp flour
½ tsp ground cinnamon
icing sugar, for dusting (optional)

Method
1. Put most (55g) of the butter and all the chocolate into a double boiler and melt completely on a low heat. Or, microwave, on High, for intervals of 30 seconds, no longer, until melted. Beat to mix.
2. In a separate bowl, whisk together the eggs, egg yolks and vanilla sugar, using an electric beater, until light, pale and thick.
3. Pour the egg mix, 2 teaspoons of the flour, and the cinnamon into the chocolate-butter mixture.
4. Using the remaining butter, coat four 150ml metal moulds, heatproof china ramekins or heatproof glass dishes. Dust in the reserved flour. Repeat this process. Spoon the chocolate brownie mix equally into the dishes.
5. Bake in an oven, preheated to 230°C/Gas 8, for 6–7 minutes, or until the top and sides look and feel set.
6. Let the cakes sit for 1 minute. Tip each one gently, on its side, and with fingers ease each little cake out onto a plate: it should be complete. Dust with icing sugar, if liked, and serve hot.

sweet biscuits

Home-baked biscuits are, of course, delicious, but some biscuits are difficult to reproduce at home, especially those with lacy, brittle or chewy textures. The classic biscuits and confections described here are made using good ingredients and can be used to create desserts in minutes.

1 Langues-de-chat These wafer-thin French biscuits line moulded fruit charlottes beautifully, and can be used to line ice cream moulds, or to sandwich tiny slices of ice cream. Layered with crème chantilly and puréed apricot, they make superb desserts.

2 Speculaas These crunchy Dutch biscuits are flavoured with ginger and cardamom. (Similar spicy biscuits exist all over Europe.) They can be used in trifles, crumbled between apples and yoghurt, or finely crushed and folded into crème fraîche.

3 Ginger thins Delicately thin and spicy, these biscuits can be crushed over baked fruits, crumbled for use in cheesecakes, or mixed with yoghurt and preserved ginger.

4 Amaretti These famous biscuits, wrapped in pairs, have a distinctive bitter almond taste and are superb in cooking. Soaked in Marsala and layered with ricotta, they make an instant pudding. Crumble them to top baked or fresh peaches, or add as a crunchy topping to puréed apricots with mascarpone.

5 Sponge fingers Also known as boudoir or savoiardi biscuits, these puffy but crisp sponge biscuits are perfect for soaking up alcohol: in trifles (dipped first into port or sherry) and tiramisu (dipped into coffee liqueur), for example.

6 Brandy snap baskets These lacy, toffee-like wafers, which can be rolled (brandy snaps) or shaped into baskets, can be filled with all sorts of delicious things, from simple whipped cream to diced pears or rum-soaked soft berries. Brushed with melted chocolate, they'll hold chocolate mousse or ice cream.

7 Marshmallows Fluffy, soft and bland, these sweet confections are a common cooking ingredient in the United States, for cakes and sweet sauces. Try folding them into melted chocolate and mixing with nuts, for a rich dessert.

8 Digestive biscuits Made with wholemeal flour, these high-fibre biscuits have a 'short', crumbly texture that is perfect for crushing for cheesecake and Banoffee pie bases. Also try them crumbled with nuts, rolled oats and butter as a baked fruit topping.

9 Biscotti Literally 'twice cooked', these Italian biscuits usually contain nuts, dried fruit or chocolate, and work beautifully in frothy egg or cream desserts. Use them, alcohol-dipped, as a basis for trifles. Crushed and softened in vin santo and mixed with ricotta and ground coffee beans, they make a scrumptious pudding.

10 Meringues These confections of egg white and sugar, though easily made, take hours to cook. Ready-made meringues are perfectly good for making ice cream sundaes or Eton Mess (crushed meringue and raspberries folded into thick cream).

preserved fruit & vegetables

dried fruit

Sweet, energy-packed and long-lasting, dried fruit are one of nature's most dazzling convenience foods. Totally versatile, they are useful in innumerable dishes, from puddings – soaked in fruit juice or alcohol, dried fruit make elegant desserts – to salads and rice dishes. Once upon a time, all we could buy were raisins, prunes and apricots, but now the choice is huge and infinitely colourful.

Avoid over-dried fruits, which can't be improved by hours of soaking, although now the fashion is more for dried fruits that are soft and 'ready to eat'. Most fruits, when dried, don't retain their colour and moisture naturally, so are coated or soaked in substances that may or may not be acceptable: always check the label. (Sulphur dioxide, used on a lot of ready-to-eat products, helps retain the fruit's colour and natural acidity but it may cause allergic reactions in asthmatics.)

1 Raisins Juicy dried grapes, raisins vary in shape, size, flavour and seed content, depending on the grape type used. Many come from California and are seedless, dark, small and glossy (a). Use these in dried fruit salads, muffins, stuffed apples and chutneys. Muscat raisins (b), made from the supersweet muscatel grape, keep some of the original bloom and are sharp-tasting. These can be plumped up in cinnamon-tea syrup, mixed with cream cheese and drizzled with muscatel wine, or used in rum and raisin ice cream. Jumbo or golden raisins are superb in rice puddings, cheesecakes and other dishes where their pale colour counts.

2 Sultanas Made from dried seedless green grapes, sultanas are paler and sweeter than raisins. Their colour and flavour changes

according to their provenance. Some suit certain uses better than others, but Californian (a), Australian (b) and South African (c) sultanas, for example, are all good in sponge puddings, sweet pastries, fruit cakes, spice breads, biscuits, curries and chutneys.

3 Currants Originally from Corinth in Greece, currants are one of the most ancient of dried vine fruits. They are tiny black grapes that, when dried, are intensely sweet but very tart. They are much used in baking, including in dried fruit mixtures for mincemeat pastries.

4 Prunes Dark, glossy and chewy, prunes are simply dried plums. Californian prunes (a) dominate the market. While the ready-to-eat versions are perfect for stuffing with blanched almonds or cream

cheese, the drier versions usually need simmering in water, wine or port, for use in meat stews, mousses and compotes. The sexiest prunes around are the plump Agen prunes (b), from France, best eaten on their own or wrapped in bacon and grilled.

5 Dates The dried fruits of a type of palm tree, and a staple food in North Africa and the Middle East, are either 'soft' (eaten fresh), 'semi-dry' (the most common) or 'hard' (rare in the West). Use semi-dry dates (a) in loaves, biscuits and steamed puddings, or cook them with orange juice to a purée for filling cakes. Fleshy Medjool dates (b), also semi-dry, are delicious eaten uncooked and filled with cheese, nuts or marzipan. Or mix them with orange flower water and sliced orange, as a salad.

6 Sour cherries These are deliciously scented, sweet and sharp, and grow fat, soft and juicy when soaked. Use them in sauces, steamed puddings and pie fillings, or soak them in Kirsch for cheesecakes.

7 Cranberries Sweet but sharp, dried cranberries add pleasing tartness and colour to all kinds of sweet and savoury foods, especially rice and yoghurt dishes, spiced pastries and fruit compotes. Try them in rich apple tart for contrast, or cook and then purée them with spiced syrup for sweet pastries.

8 Barberries These gloriously red, jewel-like fruit have a clean, sharp flavour and are a favourite Middle Eastern food. Add them to sweet rice dishes and yoghurt or cream cheese desserts, or scatter them over stewed fruits for texture, colour and acidity.

9 Apricots Dried apricots have glorious sharp-scented sweetness, colour and chewiness. Cooked, in pies or as a purée with orange flower water, or to stir into creamy desserts, they excel. For many cooks, the bright orange, sweet-sharp apricots (a) are the ideal. The 'healthier', unsulphured versions are a dark brown and have a toffee-like flavour. Dried apricots are also available in pieces (b).

10 Amardine (apricot paste sheet) Of Middle Eastern and eastern Mediterranean origin, amardine can be cut into shapes, or rolled up with marzipan as sweet sushi. Or boil it with orange juice, add sugar and orange flower water, and blend to make a drink.

11 Coconut The white meat of the coconut is available dried in various forms. Coconut shreds (a), thin slivers of coconut, are excellent mixed with brown sugar, butter and nuts as a topping for baked fruit puddings. Use them in muffins and banana loaves, or toast and crumble them over raw seafood or ceviche.

More common desiccated coconut (b), a powdery product, is useful for coconut cakes and ice cream, and to thicken curries (it is very absorbent); buy the plain rather than the sweetened version.

12 Figs Many types of dried and semi-dried figs are produced all over the Mediterranean. They are usually sold either whole (a) or pressed into cakes, which are easily broken up into individual figs (b). Because of the high sugar content, figs dry superbly well. They are wonderful in chutneys, sauces and pickles, and add lemony sweetness to stews, cakes and puddings. Miniature, white figs (c) are good added whole to meat and poultry marinades, or rehydrated in hot liquids to add to salads.

13 Fruit leathers Antipodean fruit leathers, made from dried red berry or stone fruit purée, are strong, sharp and sweet. They can be cut up with scissors and heated in water or wine to make a sauce, or used to add a brilliant fruit flavour and colour to cakes and puddings.

fruited turkey and chestnut meat loaf

This meat loaf uses minced turkey and pork in place of the usual minced beef, and has dried fruits and chestnuts to add a boost to the flavour and texture. The result is an intriguing mosaic of lean meat and fruit. Served hot, the loaf is a wonderful, celebratory autumn or winter dish, but it is also delicious served cold.

Serves 4–6

Ingredients
olive oil, for brushing
450g lean turkey (dark meat),
    minced
100g lean pork or bacon, minced
2 tbsp concentrated chicken
    bouillon
1 handful parsley and/or mixed
    fresh herbs, chopped, or 2 tsp
    dried herbs to taste
2 tbsp Worcestershire sauce
1 tsp anchovy essence
100g dried apricots or peaches
100g Agen prunes
75g dried cranberries, cherries
    or blueberries
1 slice wholemeal or granary
    bread, crumbed
1 egg, beaten
200g chestnuts, canned or
    vac-packed
200g turkey strips or goujons
salt and freshly ground black
    pepper

Method
1. First, fold a large piece of foil in half and use it to line the base and two long sides of a 1kg metal loaf tin. Leave extra foil at the sides to wrap over the top as the loaf cooks. Brush or rub the whole surface (including the short ends of the tin) with the oil.
2. Mix the turkey, pork (or bacon) and bouillon in a bowl. Add the herbs, sauces, and generous seasonings to taste.
3. Pour 100ml of boiling water over the dried fruits. Leave to soak for 10 minutes and then drain, reserving 4 tablespoons of the soaking liquid. Mix the liquid with the breadcrumbs and beat with a fork. Stir the beaten egg and then the soaked bread into the meat mixture.
4. Scissor-chop 4 each of the apricots, prunes and chestnuts, and several of the smaller fruits. Add these to the meat mixture.
5. Use some of the remaining fruits and chestnuts to line the base of the tin. Press in one-third of the meat mixture, then some turkey strips and more dried fruit and chestnuts. Repeat the process until all the ingredients are used up. Press the mixture down firmly with wetted hands, and fold the oiled foil flaps over the top, loosely.
6. Bake in an oven, preheated to 180°C/Gas 4, for 50–60 minutes, opening the foil after 40 minutes. Test the interior temperature, using a meat thermometer: it should be 71°C or so. Remove from the oven and let the loaf stand for 10 minutes.
7. Drain off any liquid that has formed. (This will turn into jelly by the next day, and can be served cold with the loaf, or used in soup.) Serve the loaf in thick slices, either hot, immediately, or chilled, the next day.

abricotines

The elegantly minimalist recipe for these sweets features in Claudia Roden's wonderful work, *The Book of Jewish Food*. To get the best results, follow her advice about choosing the fruit: "Make these with a natural – tart – variety of dried apricots, not the sweetened or honeyed ones. They must also be soft."

Makes 56

Ingredients
500g dried apricots
75g pistachios, coarsely chopped
icing sugar, for coating
a few whole pistachios, to
    decorate

Method
1. Do not soak or wash the apricots, or you will produce a cream. Put them as they are in a food processor and blend them to a smooth paste, adding a very little water, by the teaspoon, if necessary.
2. Work the chopped pistachios into the paste with your hands.
3. Wash your hands and, wetting them or greasing them with a little oil so that the paste does not stick, take little lumps of paste and roll it into marble-sized balls.
4. Roll them in icing sugar and press half a pistachio on top of each.

foods preserved in sugar or alcohol

Preservation in syrup or alcohol is usually an excellent way to conserve the plumpness and flavour of fruit, vegetables and other foods. Depending on the sweetness, flavour and shape of the original foods, they can be either eaten as they are (with yoghurt, ice cream, or rice pudding, for example), or used as part of a dessert, whether in a soufflé or tart, or as a filling for pancakes or sweet omelettes. Furthermore, the surrounding aromatic liquid is itself useful, in both sweet and savoury cooking: try using it to deglaze the pan after roasting meat, or to add to casseroles or soups.

1 Preserved ginger in syrup These fleshy, sweet-but-hot chunks of fresh ginger in syrup are great for both savoury and sweet dishes. You can pour the syrup over ice cream, or use it to flavour custards and yoghurts, and ginger can be added to cakes, biscuits or to citrus fruit salads. If you use up the syrup before the ginger, top up the jar with honey or rum.

2 Pears in wine Rosy from being soaked in ruby port, pears make excellent festive preserves to serve with game, goose or ham, or they can be stuffed with cheese or nuts as an easy dessert. Boiled down until it is sticky, the preserving liquid becomes intensely flavourful.

3 Glyka A product of Greece and Turkey, *glyka* consists of a sweet, heavy syrup in which tiny immature fruits, such as cherries and figs (pictured), are preserved whole. Beautiful, chewy and very sweet, these are an acquired taste; you may prefer to add extra acidity. Try them with yoghurt or cream cheese.

4 Clementines in alcohol Tiny oranges, such as clementines, flavour any syrup deliciously, particularly if Cognac, curaçao or whisky is added. Use the fruit and syrup in trifles or rice puddings, or stir them into thick cream.

5 Cherries in alcohol Dark cherries preserve wonderfully in a syrup containing Kirsch or white rum. Use the cherries in ice cream sundaes, in cakes, pavlova, or cheesecakes, or top the cherries and syrup with cream or yoghurt as a simple dessert. The syrup flavours smoothies superbly, too.

6 Aduki beans These tiny reddish beans, very popular in Thailand, come in a sticky-sweet and nutty syrup. The beans, mashed, can be used to fill dumplings, for steaming, which can then be served with the bean syrup. Or try whizzing the syrup up with lychee juice and rose water, add the lychees and aduki beans, and serve as a drink-cum-dessert on ice.

7 Candied orange slices These colourful slices of orange, pretty as stained-glass windows, can be used to top cheesecakes, orange cakes or lemon tarts, or to line steamed pudding bowls. Poached in wine, and then reduced, they make an ambrosial pour-over sauce.

8 Marrons glacés Sweet chestnuts, infused with a syrup and usually French, taste superb eaten with Camembert or Roquefort cheese. Or try crumbling them on top of cream, custard, yoghurt or rose-scented rice pudding.

9 Candied citron These colourful pieces of zest, from a large, lemon-like citrus fruit called citron, are infused in syrup until they become dense, leathery and amazingly sweet. Use slivers to top fruit cakes or milky puddings, or in cream cheese desserts and cheesecakes. Or offer with goat's cheese and walnuts as a salad or dessert in itself. Look for whole pieces rather than the more common fragments.

chutneys, relishes and sweet pickles

Although precise definitions vary greatly from one food culture to another, salt, vinegar, sugar and spices underpin most of the products in this category. Hot oils may also feature. These condiments add flavour, texture, crunch and pungency to rich or plain foods, and make everyday meals more interesting. Mango chutney with a curry, sweetcorn relish with a burger, or ploughman's pickle in a cheese sandwich: these pairings typify a lively culinary tradition.

1 Cranberry relish This jam-like relish is a traditional accompaniment for turkey, chicken or venison. Blend it with equal quantities of orange juice to make an appealing coulis. It also goes extremely well with salty white cheeses, such as feta.

2 Mango chutney The mango chutney so beloved in Britain is not an authentic Indian preserve, despite being a traditional accompaniment to curries. It is sweet and sour rather than hot, turmeric, ginger and garlic being the usual flavourings. Mango chutney goes well in Cheddar cheese sandwiches and in cold chicken salads. It also adds 'bite' to mango ice cream.

3 Tomato and onion chutney Often served with hamburgers or with cold meats or sausages, this sweet relish has only mild spiciness. Whisk it into two parts of softened butter as a barbecue baste for chops and steaks, or stir it into whipped cream as a dressing.

4 Mint and coriander relish This green, herb-rich preserve is a useful accompaniment for many Asian foods, particularly Thai and Vietnamese dishes. Stir it into thick yoghurt as a dressing, mix it into fish salads, or serve it with noodle or rice dishes, and coconutty curries.

5 Achards These curious pickles, found in various forms in Africa, India and Southeast Asia, are made of crunchy, chunky bits of vegetable preserved in a turmeric-flavoured pickle liquid. Use them with sliced cold meats,

poultry or fish, or to add interest to noodles and rice. The pickle liquid is also good in Asian vinaigrettes.

6 Ploughman's pickle Apple, onion and raisins usually feature in this sweet and spicy pickle. Far from subtle, it is an excellent condiment for hard British cheeses, such as Cheddar, and sausages. Mixed with soured cream and paprika, it makes a dip for chicory or apple segments.

7 Sweetcorn relish Sweet and mild, this fine-cut, syrupy relish makes a good spread for hot or cold meat sandwiches. It also goes well with cheese, poultry, salami and smoked fish, such as mackerel. Folded into curd cheese, it makes a tangy toast-topping or filling for celery sticks.

8 Lime pickle This sharp and spicy Indian pickle is usually fairly dry, with large chunks of lime and other vegetables visible in a turmeric, chilli and ginger paste. It is superb served as a side dish, with dhal, rice, curries and poppadoms, or as a refreshing, chewy foil for mild meats, poultry and fish. Stir it into a mayonnaise-based chicken salad, or add it to ham, tongue or egg sandwiches.

9 Mostarda di frutta di Cremona This Italian preserve of whole candied fruits in syrup flavoured with spicy mustard oil is delicious spooned over slices of rare beef, smoked duck breast or smoked venison. Mixed into hot roast chicken pan drippings, it creates a delicious and unusual gravy.

pickles

The use of *cornichons* in sauce tartare, of umeboshi plums in Japanese sushi and of salt-pickled lemons in Tunisian tagines has been famous for centuries. Dependent on salt, vinegar and aromatics, pickles pep up our meals, whether they are used alone as condiments or in recipes. They encourage good digestion, stimulate the palate, and keep our interest aroused.

1 Dill pickles and gherkins Small varieties of cucumber, as well as gherkins, are used for pickling. Dill pickles (a) consist of small cucumbers pickled with dill heads or seeds, peppercorns and other aromatics. Soft, mild and faintly crunchy, these go well with hard cheese and cured meats, such as pastrami and salami. The pickle liquid is also excellent added to vinaigrettes, or to soured cream to accompany smoked salmon.

Pickled gherkins or, in French, *cornichons* (b), are smaller, darker and chewier. Eat them with rich pâté and cold meats, or slice them finely as a garnish or to scatter over creamy fish or poultry dishes, to add colour and sharpness.

2 Capers The pickled buds of the Mediterranean shrub, *Capparis spinosa*, come in different sizes. Tiny *non pareilles* (a) are the most prized, and most enjoyable for their prettiness and sweet, sharp but mellow flavour. Use them in velouté or béchamel sauces for delicate white fish or poached chicken, or scatter them over mayonnaise-dressed foods. *Capucines* (b), with a loose, hood-like outer covering, are medium-sized and good for more general use: on pizzas and in sauces such as salsa verde, tartare sauce and tapenade. Salted capers (c) can

boost pasta or meat sauces, and are good with skate and black butter sauce, or pounded into herb or French dressings.

Caperberries (d), the fruits of the same plant, are fleshier, milder and sturdier than the buds. They look and taste good with hard cheeses, ham, salami and chicken. Remove the stem before chopping or blending them into mayonnaise, hollandaise sauce (for fish) or cream (for poached chicken).

3 Sauerkraut This famous German condiment is essentially dry-salted white cabbage that is preserved by its own fermentation and flavoured with spices. Use it straight, hot or cold, as a side dish, or it can be cooked with apples and white wine to accompany boiled pork.

4 Baby beetroot Young beetroot, preserved in a vinegary brine, are deliciously sweet-sharp and

colourful. Use them to accompany cured herring or, along with onion rings and dill, to embellish open sandwiches: they go well with Dutch cheeses, cold ham and smoked sausage. Liquidised with buttermilk, some pickling liquid, sliced onion and radishes, they make an instant borscht. Beetroot salsa, made with beetroot, tomato and dill, takes just seconds to make.

5 Umeboshi plums The ume in umeboshi is, in fact, a type of apricot, but because it reddens and grows sourer when pickled, the name 'plum' has stuck. Umeboshi are eaten daily in Japan, usually with breakfast rice porridge. Use them, chopped or mashed, in sushi or puréed as a dipping sauce

6 Pickled lemons Preserved in coarse salt, brine and aromatics, decorative North African pickled lemons gain an intense, sharp, spicy taste as they mature. (Beware any preserved lemons containing sodium benzoate, which creates off-flavours.) Scrape out and discard the pith and the flesh: only the zest is eaten. Use with couscous, in tagines, or as a stuffing for chicken.

7 Pickled ginger This Japanese condiment consists of paper-thin slices of ginger preserved in a sweet and sour pickle that contains shiso leaf (pink) colouring or beetroot liquid. It is the traditional

accompaniment for sushi and sashimi, along with wasabi paste and tamari. Pickled ginger can also be used in stir-fries and fish dishes.

8 Pickled samphire Found around Europe, in saltmarshes and estuaries near the sea, this slender plant is delicious fresh, but is more often sold pickled, as marsh samphire or *salicorne* (the latter from France). Pickled samphire makes an unusual condiment, salad or side dish for salted or smoked seafood. Or use it as a stuffing or sandwich filling for ham or bacon.

9 Mustard greens Pickled mustard greens, of which there are many different variations all over China, have an evil aroma but taste delicious as a condiment. Many are made from

brassicas, such as bok choy or choy sum, and sometimes radish is included. Use them with rice or noodle dishes, or in stuffings for spring rolls, rice paper wraps or steamed buns.

10 Pickled walnuts These black, sharp-tasting orbs are immature walnuts that have been pickled in a seasoned vinegar. Chewy and astringent, they make a good foil for rich meats, such as roast goose or duck, or strong cheeses. Chop them into pale chicken, rice or pasta salads for contrast, or wrap them in cured ham and puff pastry, and then bake: superb.

11 Torshi left These luminous pink turnip pieces, in a sharp, sweet beetroot pickling liquid, are famous in Egypt, Syria and Lebanon. They have a superb spiciness and apple-like crunch. Try them in flatbread wraps, with white cheese, chillies and lettuce; in a chickpea salad with rice, fresh coriander and olive oil; or in an onion and beetroot salad with toasted cumin seeds.

12 Kimchi To Koreans, this hot, sour-tasting pickled cabbage is an essential condiment. There are numerous variations using vegetables such as radish or cucumber, but true kimchi contains only Chinese cabbage. Kimchi is delicious served with beef and veal dishes, tofu stir-fries, squid, and noodles. The pickle ingredients themselves – including ginger, red chilli and preserved oysters and/or shrimp – lend particular pungency.

chicken tagine with pickled lemons

This somewhat Westernised North African stew is beautifully fragrant with fruits, spices and exotic flavourings, shot through with the sharp and spicy intensity of the pickled lemons.

Serves 4–6

Ingredients

400g boneless chicken thigh fillets, skinned, halved

1 onion, cut into 8 but left joined at the base

4 tbsp chermoula spice paste (see page 14)

2 tsp turmeric powder

2 tbsp extra virgin olive oil or argan oil

8 each of dried figs, apricots and mango slices

1 apple or pear, cut into segments and cored

450ml chicken stock or water, boiling

2 tbsp dried scented rose petals (optional)

1 salt-pickled lemon, in quarters

½ tsp rose water or orange flower water

salt

Method

1. Rub the chicken and onion segments all over with the chermoula spice paste and turmeric.

2. Heat the oil in a large heatproof nonreactive pan (glazed ceramic or metal) and brown the chicken and onion well. Then add the dried fruits, apple, stock and rose petals, if using.

3. Scrape away and discard the flesh and pith from the pickled lemon. Add the peel to the pan and bring the contents to near boiling, then lower the heat and simmer for 25–35 minutes, or until the juices are syrupy, the chicken tender, the fruit soft, and the flavours well integrated.

4. Season well with salt: the sweetness needs balancing. Serve hot with couscous tossed with a little argan oil, salt and black pepper.

fruit fool in filo pastry cups

The appeal of these delicate desserts depends on the crispness of the filo pastry and the lightness of the creamy filling, which is enlivened by the intense fruit flavours of the vodka-infused blackcurrants.

Serves 4

Ingredients
1 large sheet filo pastry
25g salted butter, melted
1 tsp scented clear honey
100g jar blackcurrants in vodka
   syrup, strained, liquid reserved
200ml double cream, chilled

Method
1. Cut the filo pastry sheet into 8 equal squares, using scissors. Take 4 muffin tins and place 2 filo squares in each, at right angles, so that 8 points stick up. Push the sheets down firmly to create cups.
2. Bake at 180°C/Gas 4 for 20–30 minutes or until golden. Mix the butter and honey together and use this mixture to brush the pastry cups before returning them to the oven. Bake for 10 minutes more, and then leave to cool.
3. Slightly crush some of the blackcurrants. Whip the cream until stiff peaks form, then fold in the strained fruit and some of their syrup.
4. Spoon the fruit-cream fool into the filo cups with some syrup spooned over or around, as well, if liked. Eat immediately, while the textures and tastes are at their most pristine.

dried vegetables

Although less essential than in the past, dried vegetables are still a practical addition to any store-cupboard, as long as you buy those with decent taste, texture, colour and aroma. Today's dried vegetables fall into two main categories: the 'luxury exotics', which include sea vegetables (seaweeds), and the ultra-convenient soup mix or pasta sauce packs, which come ready-mixed. Food-processed or pounded, these last two can be used to thicken sauces or add interest to pasta or rice, or they can be mixed with sea salt flakes and crushed pepper as a creative seasoning.

3 Mixed vegetables This mix is the basis of many inferior packet soup mixes worldwide. However, a good-quality, chunky and aromatic mix, added to tomato, chicken or mixed vegetable soups, can quickly boost flavour, colour and taste; allow time for full rehydration. Ground to a powder, the mix can thicken and enrich pasta sauces.

4 Vegetable crisps Reputable brands of vegetable crisps, which contain colourful vegetables such as blue potato, beetroot and carrot, make a novel crispy topping on gratin dishes or baked fish, if crushed. Or crush them into cream cheese with garlic as a dip.

5 Nori The best-known Japanese seaweed, nori is made from a red seaweed that is reduced to a pulp and then dried like paper. It is used as a wrap for sushi, but it can also be torn into bits or scissor-shredded, for use in cold noodle salads, or as a texture-colour-taste booster for pasta dishes.

6 Wakame This fine, slightly pleated brown seaweed, which turns green in boiling liquids, has a delicate texture, and adds appeal to textural Asian dishes in which a mild sea salt tang is useful: for example, in prawn or squid dishes, and noodle or rice dishes. Dry, it can be ground to a powder and sprinkled into or over fine noodle dishes.

7 Arame These thin, brittle seaweed shreds are brilliantly useful to add to seafood dishes at the start of cooking; they hydrate to wiry, chewy strands, with a salty-sweet taste. Added to rice, noodles and even vegetable stews, casseroles or soups, they provide contrast and body, as well as a taste of the sea.

8 Kombu (konbu) Once rehydrated in boiling water or stock, this ribbon-like seaweed turns soft and chewy, and has an intense sea salt savour. It boosts fish stocks, seafood stews and Japanese fish-rice dishes, and is essential for authentic sushi rice. If used in stir-fries, it must be fully presoaked first. Kombu can also be used as a flavourant that is removed (as for bouquet garni).

1 Sun-dried tomatoes When dried, tomatoes (technically fruits) are wonderfully meaty and sweet, with a sharp aftertaste. The leather-dry tomatoes sold in packets (as opposed to those packed in oil) are the most versatile. Rehydrate them in boiling stock, then slice them into pasta sauces or salads. Or whiz them up with garlic, olive oil, anchovies and stock as a spread.

2 Arrabbiata capsicum mix This strong-flavoured mix of dried chillies and sweet peppers (sometimes with milder additions, such as courgette) is extremely useful. Rehydrated, it can be sprinkled into soups, or used in pasta or rice sauces to add sweetness, hotness and colour. Or use it with oil and lemon juice as an instant dressing or marinade.

squid, noodle and seaweed salad

When rehydrated, dried seaweed has an alluring scent and taste of the sea, intriguing chewy texture and curious colours. This salad makes the most of all these features, adding the sweetness of squid, chilli and garlic.

Serves 4–6

Ingredients
25g dried wakame sheets
25g dried arame strips
25g dried hijiki shreds
100g wide dried rice noodles
12 small fresh squid (about 350g)
1 tbsp chilli oil
2 tsp roasted sesame oil
1 tbsp avocado oil
2 garlic cloves, chopped
1cm chunk fresh ginger, peeled
 and shredded
juice of 1 lemon or lime
sea salt, crushed, and freshly
 ground black pepper
1 tbsp seaweed seasoning
 (optional)

Method
1. Put all the dried seaweed into a colander placed in a heatproof bowl. Pour enough near-boiling water over it to cover. Leave to soak for 5–8 minutes, or until the seaweed is plump, fleshy and softened. Lift out of the colander, leaving the liquid in the bowl, and rinse in cold water.
2. Add the rice noodles to the hot liquid in the bowl. Leave to soften, and then drain while still firm. Rinse the noodles in cold water and add them to the seaweed.
3. Prepare the squid: trim off and keep the tentacles; discard the eye section, including the beak, empty the gut contents and discard the clear backbone or quill. Slice open the squid, and make score marks in a criss-cross pattern on the skin side of half of them.
4. Heat the oils, garlic and ginger in a large frying pan. Add the squid and stir-fry for 1–2 minutes or until opaque and tender. Toss in the drained seaweed and noodles, add the lemon juice and seasonings, and serve.

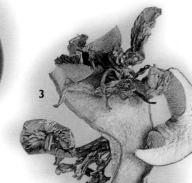

mushrooms

Not only does drying enable us to use a range of mushrooms that are unavailable fresh, but dried mushrooms are an extremely useful source of flavour and texture in everything from sauces to pasta and rice dishes. Certain mushrooms, such as ceps and morels, are outstanding when dried, meaty and intensely strong in flavour. Some, such as wood ear mushrooms, are prized mainly for their texture and appearance, while others, such as chanterelles, have a defined, if modest taste. Most dried mushrooms need soaking in hot water, but the resultant stock can often be used in the cooking.

Bottled and canned mushrooms retain their flavour less well than their dried counterparts, but are often pleasantly textural. Use onion, garlic, fresh herbs, spices, or Asian flavours such as soy sauce to bring out the mushrooms' flavour.

dried mushrooms

1 Wood ear (Black fungus) The best Auricularia ('ear') mushrooms, often Chinese, are thin, tiny and black all over. When rehydrated, they magically balloon out and are silky and delicately chewy. Wood ears are good stir-fried or steamed, or added to Asian-style stews and noodle or rice dishes.

2 Fairy-ring mushrooms These tiny mushrooms are superb in clear soups and creamy sauces. Not as intensely flavoured as many wild mushrooms, they suit quenelles, beignets, ravioli and white poultry and fish mousses. Do not overwhelm them by using with boisterous wines.

3 Mixed mushrooms Dried mushroom mixtures often contain a poor mix of undistinguished fungi such as oyster and chestnut mushrooms. Look for 'woodland mix' selections, including ceps, morels and fairy-ring

mushrooms. Use in soups, sauces, stuffings for pancakes, ravioli and omelettes, and in casseroles and pasta sauces.

4 Chanterelles (girolles) Usually French or Italian, these delicious mushrooms range from small, pale, delicate specimens to dark-gilled large ones. Rehydrate them in hot broth or wine, and add garlic, herbs and maybe Marsala, butter, olive oil or cream for extra richness. They work beautifully in fricassees, soups, sauces, risottos and pasta dishes.

5 Morels These prized black-capped fungi are almost better dried than fresh. Rehydrate them in hot stock or wine, and add butter or olive oil, garlic and herbs: use this as a base for a delicate soup or as a sauce for chicken breast, white

fish, pasta, risotto or polenta. Ground to a powder, dried morels can season soups and risottos.

6 Ceps (Boletus) Of the various types of cep, it is the classic French cep, *Boletus edulis*, that is the most prized. Look for unbroken slices, although smaller pieces are fine if all you want is flavour. Beware cultivated Asian ceps with no smell; the best are usually from France or Italy (where ceps are known as *porcini*). Use them, rehydrated in white wine or stock, in soups and sauces for poultry, meat, vegetables, polenta and pasta, or in risottos.

7 Shiitake These cultivated Asian fungi with speckled caps and inedible stalks rehydrate to plump vegetables with a pleasing chewy 'bite' and slightly sulphurous taste. Use them, soaked, to add taste and texture to vegetable stir-fries and chicken stews, or to garnish clear, flavourful broths.

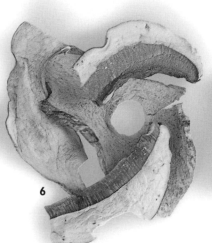

canned or bottled mushrooms

1 Ceps Bottled ceps, such as the Polish variety pictured, should be plump, brightly coloured and fairly intact. Heated gently, with olive oil, onion and garlic, they are delicious served on toast. Or cook them, sliced, with cream, wine and herbs as an appetiser, an accompaniment, part of a sauce, or puréed in rich broth as a velvety soup.

2 Mixed wild mushrooms Bottled wild (or 'forest') mushrooms should comprise a tasty assortment of fungi, such as ceps, morels, straw and pied de mouton mushrooms. Sauté them in garlicky butter, goose fat or olive oil, scatter with parsley and then use them on toast, as a sauce for pasta, rice or polenta, or as part of a braised pork dish.

3 Straw mushrooms These Asian (usually Chinese) mushrooms are softly chewy and quite delicate. Drain off the preserving liquid (this is rarely well flavoured) and heat the mushrooms in peanut oil, with ginger, garlic and herbs, or add them to clear chicken or vegetable soups, stir-fries or fine noodle or tofu dishes for texture and colour. They also taste good combined with bamboo shoots, bean sprouts and spring onions in fritters or omelettes.

4 Black truffles Bottled truffles may lack the glorious aroma and taste of the fresh variety, but they are still useful as long as you buy whole truffles. Use them sliced and heated (in truffle oil, chicken stock, wine or

other flavourful liquid), as a novel garnish for chicken breast or white fish fillets, or on poached or soft-boiled eggs. Or slice them and mash them up with garlic, lemon juice, salted butter and parsley for steaks, chicken breasts, pasta or grilled white fish.

5 Chanterelles (girolles) Often French or Italian, but found all over Europe, these delicious mushrooms can be delicately savoury or strong in flavour. Heat them in butter, olive oil, duck or goose fat, with garlic and onions, add wine, rich stock or cream (and a splash of Marsala, if liked), and use in rice or noodle dishes, soups, sauces or soufflés, with chicken, veal or lamb.

vegetables in oil, brine or juice

Relatively few of us know the pleasure of strolling down the garden to pick a bundle of vine leaves or pluck a ripe red pepper straight from the plant. So we should celebrate the fact that such good, interesting vegetables are now available in bottles, cans or packets. Add a squeeze of lemon, some sizzling, garlicky butter, vinaigrette or mayonnaise, and a delicious snack, salad or meal may be just around the corner. And don't throw away the processing liquid without tasting it: when good, this can enhance soups, stews, glazes, sauces and marinades. Always look for authentic products, with adequate information about their provenance and suggested uses.

1 Vine leaves Even when blanched and brined, grape vine leaves keep their perfect shape and texture. Often Greek or Turkish in origin, the leaves can be used to wrap all sorts of foods, including semi-cooked or cooked rice mixtures, minced cooked meats, and even fish balls. Cook or heat stuffed vine leaves through thoroughly in lemony stock, and then drizzle them with extra virgin olive oil.

2 Roasted sweet peppers Superbly succulent sweet peppers (or pimiento), from the Mediterranean, preserve beautifully after roasting; the sweet, oily syrup in which they are sold is often delicious, too. In salads, they are the ultimate easy ingredient, even served with just olive oil and garlic. They are lovely in soups and purées, or sliced into pasta or rice. Or stuff them with salt cod purée, cheese mixtures or garlicky potato.

3 Aubergines in oil Sliced, char-grilled aubergines packed in good olive oil or vinaigrette can be tasty,

useful and time-saving. Use them in salads with tuna, capers and olives, or with beans. Purée them with garlic, parsley and hummus and use as a spread, or slice them into ribbons to mix with chilli-hot satay dressing and serve on rice.

4 Cherry peppers These miniature and mildly hot capsicums usually come from Hungary, Spain or South Africa. Packed in sweetish brine or oil, they stay pert, chewy and colourful. They are best eaten whole, as an appetiser with salty white cheese, mixed with olives, or as part of a salad. Served with cured meats, they make an excellent brunch dish.

5 Artichoke hearts Since artichokes need extensive preparation, canned or bottled artichoke hearts are very convenient. They are available either whole or halved; beware of unlined cans, which can leave the artichokes with a metallic taste. Simply add lemony dressings or aioli, or mix the hearts with tuna and mayonnaise as a salad. Puréed in stock and cream

with tarragon, artichoke hearts can be transformed into a quick soup.

6 Passata This tasty, semi-thick purée of tomatoes is sold under many different names worldwide, usually in bottles or cartons. The best, often Mediterranean or American, can be delicious enough to drink straight and is always useful to keep on hand to add body, colour and sweetness to savoury dishes. Use it in risotto, baked with pasta, or even, if well seasoned, as soup.

7 Plum tomatoes Though not comparable to fresh tomatoes, canned plum tomatoes add colour and are super-convenient. Use them in stews, bakes, soups, sauces and blended drinks.

Usually made from Roma or other fleshy plum tomatoes, they come either chopped (a) or whole and peeled (b). Avoid those in brine – the tastiest come packed in juice; and avoid those with added herbs or spices: it's best to add your own seasonings.

8 Sweetcorn kernels Preserved in light brine, sweet and mild sweetcorn kernels (niblets) are a useful addition to many protein-high dishes, and salads. Food-process them to a purée with garlic, onion, butter and paprika, and serve as mash, or liquidise them with stock, cream, bacon, chilli and cooked potatoes as chowder.

9 Palm hearts These young leaf shoots of certain types of palm tree are prized for their silky texture and delicacy. Use them in a salad with vinaigrettes or in

ceviche. Wrap them in prosciutto or bacon and bake; slice them into rounds and stir-fry; or add them to rich poultry or meat dishes for colour and texture.

10 Bamboo shoots These silky, mild-tasting Chinese vegetables are best bought whole rather than in slices. Drain and slice them into chunky diagonals or quarters to use in stir-fries, rice or noodles, or halve them and add them to chicken stews. They work well in satay dishes, green or red Thai curries, and hot-sour dishes.

11 Water chestnuts These popular Chinese tubers, available peeled and whole in cans, are crisp and mildly sweet-tasting, and add pleasing texture and taste to stir-fries, noodle and rice dishes, fritters, pancakes and spring rolls. More unusually, try them in a salad with spring onions, chilli and a garlicky sesame and rice wine dressing.

Water chestnuts can also add crunch to omelettes, chicken stews and pork dishes, especially with aniseed or Sichuan pepper seasonings.

wild mushroom, potato and prosciutto gratin

In this dish from Paul Gayler, celebrated chef at London's Lanesborough Hotel, dried mushrooms are used to flavour a creamy gratin: "One of my favourite gratins, full of flavour and delicately creamy", says Paul. "The prosciutto could be replaced with smoked ham, which is equally delicious."

Serves 4

Ingredients
15g dried morels
15g dried ceps
25g unsalted butter
2 shallots, finely chopped
1 garlic clove, crushed
50g prosciutto, finely diced
1 tsp thyme leaves, freshly picked
400g waxy potatoes, washed,
    unpeeled
600ml double cream
salt, freshly ground black pepper
    and nutmeg
15g freshly grated Parmesan

Method
1. Reconstitute the dried mushrooms in hand-hot water for 30 minutes, and drain well.
2. Heat the butter in a frying pan, add the mushrooms and cook over high heat for 4–5 minutes; add the shallots, garlic, prosciutto and thyme and cook for 2–3 minutes longer. Transfer the mixture to a bowl.
3. Slice the potatoes thinly and place in a large bowl. Bring the cream to the boil and pour it over the potatoes, season with salt, pepper and nutmeg, and toss well together.
4. Remove enough potatoes from the cream to make a single layer in the bottom of a well-buttered, shallow baking dish approximately 20–24cm in diameter.
5. Sprinkle some of the mushroom mixture over, then top with more potatoes. Continue to layer until all the potatoes are used up. Pour any remaining cream over just to cover. Scatter over a final layer of mushroom mixture and dust with the Parmesan cheese.
6. Bake in the oven, preheated to 190°C/Gas 5, for about 1 hour, until the top is golden and bubbly, and the potatoes are cooked so that a slender knife can be easily inserted through all the layers. Remove from the oven and allow to stand for 5 minutes before serving.

mackerel salad niçoise-style

Although far from the classic salade niçoise, this version is hugely appealing in its marriage of creamy smoked mackerel with the sharpness of the pickled and marinated vegetables. Additions such as parsley, red onion rings and cucumber can be included at will.

Serves 4

Ingredients
2 fillets smoked mackerel (about 250g)
12 crisp and curly lettuce leaves
2 freshly hard-boiled eggs, quartered
24 green or black salt-cured olives (or a mixture)
150g marinated globe artichoke hearts, quartered

4 tbsp salted or pickled capers, rinsed
2 tbsp pickled cornichons (gherkins), sliced
4 marinated sun-dried tomatoes, cut into strips
4 tbsp extra virgin olive oil
1 tbsp cornichon pickling liquid or caper vinegar

Method
1. Flake the mackerel into chunky chevrons, discarding the skin. Set to one side.
2. Tear up the lettuce and then arrange it in the bottoms of individual salad bowls, followed by some egg quarters.
3. Scatter in the remaining solid ingredients, adding the fish last.
4. Whisk together the olive oil and the cornichon pickling liquid or vinegar. Serve the salad chilled with the dressing drizzled over.

olives

The Mediterranean has long been the major source of most eating olives, but other countries, from Morocco to Mexico, have their own olive cultures. The name of a table olive variety, such as Nyons or Kalamata, generally defines its place of origin or the olive's particular characteristics, but precise definitions are tricky; many olives are sold simply as 'green' (unripe) or 'black' (ripe).

There is not a right or wrong way when it comes to choosing olives: buy those that you most enjoy. Bear in mind, however, that tiny olives suit pizza, for example, while fat, soft squashy ones make great pastes and spreads. Almost all olives are good as appetisers, served with crusty bread and olive oil, with salami or prosciutto, or other appropriate foods.

Avoid unshiny, perfectly shaped black olives in a jet-black liquid: such indifferent products are picked too early and 'cured' using metallic reagents: not ideal. Whenever possible, taste olives before you buy them since they spoil very easily, even when shop-bought.

1 Kalamata olives Named after the area of Greece from which they come, Kalamata olives are glossy, firm and salty. Stir them into tomato-based stews, bake them with whole fish, or add them to a classic Greek salad.

2 Nyons olives These tiny, chewy, black Provençal olives are used, most famously, to decorate pissaladière and pizza. They are delicious in ratatouille and in tuna and goat's cheese salads, or just plain with crusty bread and olive oil.

3 Moroccan black olives These dryish, chewy olives, which you can buy in bitingly hot harissa marinade, go well with sardines and anchovies, and in vegetable tagines.

4 Italian green olives These large, fleshy olives taste clean and fresh and have a crunchy texture. Crush them lightly and marinate them in hot olive oil with coriander and fennel seeds, crushed garlic and dried red chilli flakes: delicious.

5 Oven-dried Provençal olives These soft, wrinkly olives are available either green or black (pictured), and are the true taste of Provence. Oven-dried, often salt-cured, and with Provençal herbs added, they have an intense, dry richness. Easily squeezed to remove the pits, these olives are perfect party food. Try them with

pasta, in fish stuffings with fennel and lemon, or use them for tapenade.

6 Lucques olives These splendidly pert, angle-nosed green olives, often available in the south of France and North Africa, have a lean, dense and meaty flesh. Add them to tomato and aubergine dishes, or use them in Moroccan-style salads, with orange, red onion, orange flower water and cardamom, for example. Chopped, they make excellent green olive paste with lemon juice, garlic and oil.

7 Greek Volos olives These plump, purplish olives come from the Greek mainland town of Volos and are often packed in fruity olive oil with peppercorns and oregano.

Less sharp than Kalamata olives, they are excellent all-purpose olives. Use them as part of a mezze. Easily crushed and pitted, they are good in pureés or as a stuffing, with extra garlic and parsley, for rolled lamb.

8 Stuffed olives Spanish green olives, particularly firm and mildly salty Manzanilla olives, are some of the world's finest. Stuffed with tiny chillies (a), lemon zest (b), anchovy fillet pieces (c) or almonds (d), they make perfect tapas. Or use them in rice dishes, or in chicken, seafood or pork stews.

preserved
meat, game,
poultry & fish

sausages and salamis

The tradition of our ancestors to let nothing go to waste when a pig was butchered led to the creation of many delicious products, of which sausages and salamis are prime examples.

A mixture of lean and fat meat, dry-cured and chopped to various degrees of coarseness, and then stuffed into natural gut casings and matured, salamis come in innumerable variations. The best come from France, Italy and Spain and take time and skill to make. Sadly, most imported salamis are industrial versions of the real thing. Just because a salami is called Milano, doesn't mean that it comes from Milan. Beware luridly coloured, over seasoned salamis that have artificial casings and a soapy taste. Pick expensive salamis, which are irregular in size or in the distribution of the lean and fat meat. A good deli is more likely to sell authentic salamis than a supermarket.

Good-quality salamis, often flavoured with garlic, pepper and spices, are delicious eaten as part of an antipasto, with gherkins, sun-dried tomatoes or other accompaniments, but they can also be useful additions to salads and simple cooked dishes. Other sausages, such as cotechino and boudin blanc, are ready-cooked rather than cured, and just need reheating before eating.

1 Saucisson sec This French dry-cured pork sausage often comes in a loop shape, inside an edible gut casing that may have a layer of whitish bloom. It is dense, waxy and mild, and may be smoked. It is eaten raw and thinly sliced, usually as part of an hors d'oeuvre. It also works well in a leafy salad, with black olives.

2 Salame Milano A mixture of pork and beef or veal, this mellow-tasting salami is often mass-produced. Cube it into potato or leafy salads, or serve it as part of a cold meats platter.

3 Salame Napoletano This classic spicy salami, made from either pure pork or a mix of pork and beef, contains hot red pepper, which gives it its characteristic hotness, sharpness and balanced sweet taste. Use it on pizza, with roasted red peppers and anchovies, or to spice up a tomato, mozzarella and basil salad.

4 Salame di Veneto This attractively dappled, deep red salami is mellow and sweetly aromatic. It makes superb sandwiches with rocket, black pepper and olive oil.

5 Salame Felino Distinguished by its ties and slightly uneven, bulbous shape, this highly regarded Italian salami is flavoured with peppercorns, garlic and white wine. It is soft pink when cut and mild-tasting. Serve it, thinly sliced, with raw fennel and olives, drizzled with olive oil. Or team it with radicchio, red onions, caper-berries and a spoonful of mascarpone.

6 Luganega This Italian uncooked, cured country pork sausage, flavoured with coriander, pepper and red wine, is also made in Greece, where it is known as *lukanika*. Sold coiled in vacuum packs, it can be grilled, barbecued or fried, and served, cut in pieces, as a mezze or antipasto. Removed from the casings, and cooked with garlic, olive oil, bay leaves and wine, luganega makes a superb pasta sauce. Alternatively, serve it grilled whole with sautéed potatoes.

7 Smoked boiling sausage This mild, soft-textured cooked sausage, often sold in a U-shape or coiled, comes in many styles. If the sausage is truly smoked (and not simply 'smoke flavoured' with chemicals), it has a distinctive taste. German varieties tend to be denser, darker and most flavourful, and are superb in soups, stews and potato dishes.

8 Black pudding This blood sausage exists in various guises all over Europe: British black pudding, French *boudin noir* and Spanish *butifarra* are the best-known versions. With additions such as pork fat, onions and spices, it can taste superb. Already cooked, black pudding is easy to prepare: slice and sauté it with bacon and eggs, or use it with bacon in white bean stews.

9 Boudin blanc Creamy-textured 'white pudding' is made all over Europe, but French *boudin blanc* is particularly prized. Usually made of veal, pork and chicken, sometimes of fish, *boudin blanc* may also be flavoured with truffle (pictured). It is ready-cooked, so simply needs reheating briefly: poach or steam the sausage whole before slicing. Use it in bean or cabbage stews, in salads with bacon and egg, or in potato dishes.

10 Cotechino This famous plump and tender pork sausage from Italy is usually sold ready-cooked with seasoned lentils in a vacuum-packed bag: all it needs is reheating. Popular at Christmas and New Year, it can be eaten plain, drizzled with olive oil, or served cooked, but cold, as a salad, with vinaigrette.

11 Lap cheung These rough-textured sausages from China are mild, sweet and spicy, and consist mainly of pork. Since they are only lightly cured, they should always be cooked thoroughly. If using whole, boil them for at least 10 minutes.

Or slice and steam, sauté or stir-fry them before adding to vegetable or chicken dishes. Use them in rice and noodle dishes, in stir-fries, or minced in wraps and dumplings.

12 Chorizo This delicious, chewy, paprika-spiced pork sausage from Spain comes in many sizes, colours and strengths. It may be bought either cooked or uncooked. The ready-to-eat chorizo (a) is superb served with cheese and olives, or added to salads or piperade. The uncooked chorizo (b) can be cooked with beans, potatoes or rice, or added to soups and salads, to add spice and colour. When cooking or heating chorizo, the sausage oozes a gorgeous red, spicy oil which can be used as a dressing.

13 Kabanos Coarsely cut, dense and chewy, these cured (and often smoked) pork sausages from Poland are delicious sliced and added to omelettes, soups or bakes, or to a beetroot and red onion salad.

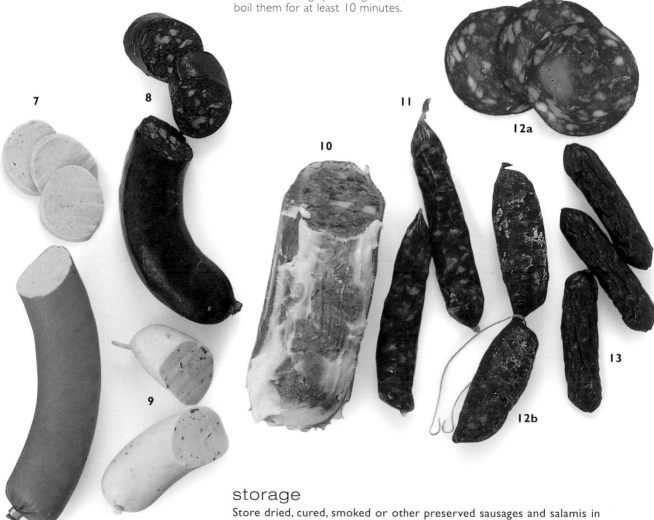

7   8   11   12a   10   9   13   12b

storage

Store dried, cured, smoked or other preserved sausages and salamis in a cool, dark, dry place, ideally unwrapped or in loose waxed paper wrappers. Most, once cut, should be refrigerated. Others keep well on cool pantry shelves. Always cut whole salamis at the time of use.

ham and bacon

Ham and bacon are both cured pork: the ham is the hind leg, while bacon is from the loin or rib areas. The curing is either wet, where the meat is soaked in brine, or dry, where salt (or saltpetre) and seasonings are rubbed into the meat: this last method is the more traditional and slower, and is far superior.

Cured 'raw' hams, such as Parma ham, are dry-cured and then air-dried, and tend to be silky and sweet, and are usually eaten thinly sliced. Hams that are cured and then cooked are paler, denser and firmer, and mild in flavour. A dry or wet cure, the salts and sugars used in the cure, slow or quick maturation, the type of wood used for smoking – all these things affect the taste, look, texture and usability of the final product.

1 York ham Dry cured and then baked, York ham tastes sweet, mild and salty. If bought sliced straight from the bone, it is most likely to have been traditionally cured. Slivers added to creamy pasta sauces, potato dishes and omelettes are delicious, and it also tastes great in scrambled eggs.

2 Kasseler Generally thought of as Polish, versions of this are made all over Europe, such as *lomo ahumado*, from Spain. Kasseler is lean meat pork loin, that is cured and then smoked. Rosy pink and very tender, with hardly any visible fat, Kasseler is best sliced wafer-thin and eaten plain.

3 Black Forest ham This delicious, raw cured German ham is firm but tender, assertively smoky and delicately sweet. It is delicious eaten alone or with warm potatoes.

4 Parma ham (prosciutto di Parma) The king among raw hams (*prosciutto crudo*), made in and around Parma in Italy, is cured in salt, massaged and hung for up to a year. Other Italian raw hams, such as Prosciutto di San Daniele, can be almost as good. Real Parma ham is too good to cook: eat it straight, wrapped around asparagus, or draped over melon.

5 Serrano ham (jamón serrano) This fine, air-dried mountain ham is made in southwestern Spain, most famously in Jabugo. The unhurried curing process produces a deep, elegant flavour, rosy colour and sweetness. Try it with membrillo, olives or slivers of goat's cheese.

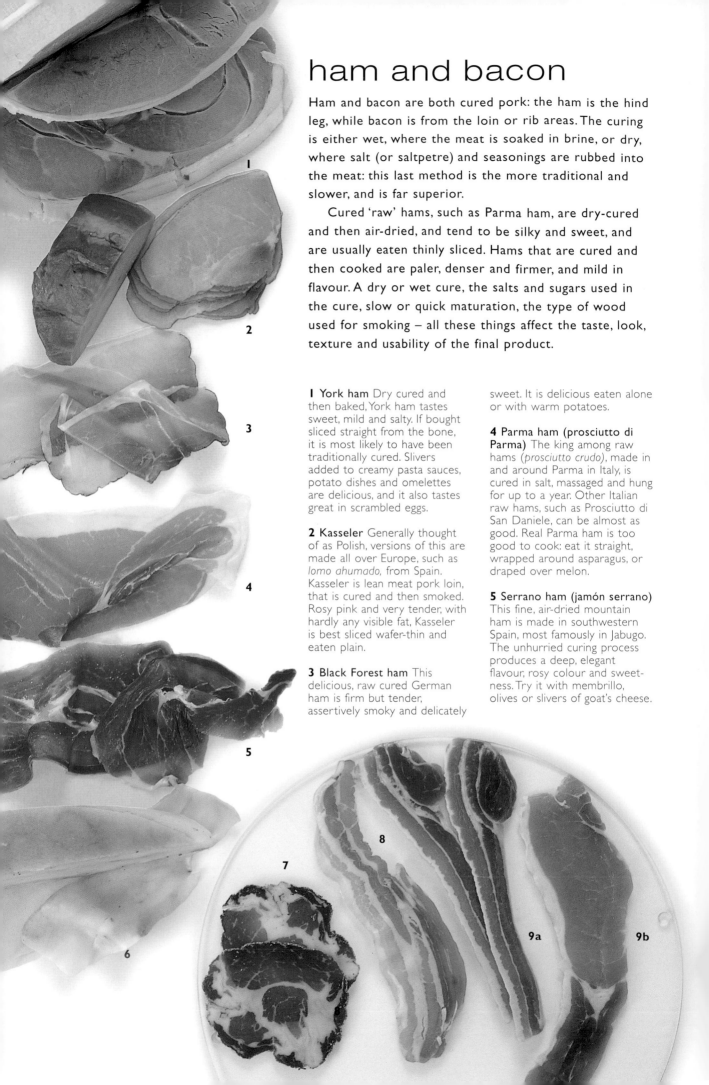

6 Lardo (speck, tocino)
Consisting almost entirely of fat, this creamy, dense and flavourful salt-cured bacon is made in Italy (where it is known as *lardo*), Germany (*speck*) and Spain (*tocino*).

Often sliced thinly and eaten raw on coarse bread, it is also wonderful to cook with. When heated, it renders an aromatic fat that is superb for sautéing potatoes. It can also add moisture and flavour to minced meat mixtures.

7 Coppa This Italian cured collar of pork (the meat is pressed into sausage skins and then hung to dry and mature) is much fattier, and therefore cheaper, than *prosciutto crudo*. Delicious sliced wafer-thin and eaten as an antipasto, it also goes well, scissor-chopped, in pasta sauces or polenta.

8 Pancetta This delicious Italian bacon, cured with herbs and spices, rolled and then pressed between boards that flatten it to a bloc or sold as a roll, is either smoked or unsmoked.

Buy it in a piece and dice it or slice it thinly, to use with spaghetti, garlic and cream, or in tomato-caper sauces for pasta. Wrap thin slices of pancetta around chicken breast pieces, white fish or oysters and bake until crisp.

9 Bacon The quality of bacon varies enormously, depending on whether it is factory- or farm-produced. The former is made by injecting brine into the meat, which speeds up production but means that lots of water is released into the pan as the bacon cooks; and the smoke flavour of factory-smoked bacon is usually synthetic. Farm bacon is more likely to be dry-cured, which produces a far superior flavour.

Fatty streaky bacon (a) can be sizzled in its own fat until crisp, and is fantastic added to pasta, gnocchi, potatoes or rice. Back bacon (b) is a leaner product and is delicious fried, grilled or baked. Serve it with sautéed apple rings; with liver; with white or black pudding; or with waffles and maple syrup.

olive-studded pork loin with pancetta and bresaola

This elegant, lean pork roast, studded with almond-stuffed olives, has a wrap of smoked pancetta for salty moistness, bresaola for sweetness and colour, and fresh rosemary for aroma and balance. A rocket salad and orzo pasta are good accompaniments.

Serves 4–6

Ingredients
550g pork loin, boned, skinned, fat removed
12 almond-stuffed green olives
sea salt and ground black pepper
2 garlic cloves, crushed to a purée
12 thin slices smoked pancetta (or smoked streaky bacon)
8 thin slices bresaola (cured beef)
1 sprig fresh rosemary
2 tbsp extra virgin olive oil
75ml Pinot Noir or other robust red wine
15g knob salted butter

Method
1. Pat dry the pork using kitchen paper. Push a knife blade into the meat at regular intervals, and insert an olive into each hole. Rub the pork all over with the crushed sea salt, pepper and garlic.
2. Lay slices of pancetta so that they overlap along the length of the pork. Then wrap around bresaola slices, until the meat is fully covered.
3. Using kitchen string, tie the pork in 4 places. Push the rosemary sprig under the string. Set on a baking tray and drizzle with olive oil.
4. Roast in an oven, preheated to 190°C/Gas 5, for 40–55 minutes, or until a meat thermometer inserted near the centre registers 72°C. Remove, cover with foil and leave to rest.
5. Place the roasting pan over high heat and pour in the wine, stirring. Add the butter and swirl to mix into a reduced, deglazed sauce.
6. Carve the meat into 1cm thick slices and serve it, hot or cold, with a drizzle of the sauce on top or alongside.

preserves and confits of meat, poultry and game

Preserved and cured meats, like many gourmet foods, evolved out of necessity. But such is the desirability of the pronounced flavours, firmer textures and appealing colours of these meats that we still produce them, even though a long shelf life is of less importance in our modern era. Even so, the fact that you can have a stock of canned or vac-packed meats in your larder or fridge means that a delectable meal is always near to hand. As well as making perfect uncooked appetisers, they can also add immense cachet to cooked main dishes.

Air- and smoke-drying, salting, sugar-curing and the use of fats, spices and herbs, along with precise and skilful treatment, ensure that these artisanal products remain tasty and convenient, long after production. When buying, look for a clearly identifiable regional provenance, which should guarantee good and consistent quality and identity.

1 Pâté de campagne Good coarse 'country pâté' is made of a balanced mix of lean and fat cooked meat, such as pork or game. Sealed with a layer of jelly or fat, terrines or pâtés keep for weeks in a cool, dark place. Eat pâté straight with bread and coarse mustard, or use it in a salad with cooked potatoes.

2 Foie gras The finest of the many grades of fattened goose or duck liver is foie gras 'entier' (or whole pieces), but foie gras 'en bloc' is also excellent and cheaper: liver pieces are marinated in sugar, salt and port or Sauternes, and then cooked to a silken-smooth texture in cans or jars. (Avoid the foie gras parfaits or purées, which are bulked out with other products.) Eat foie gras, chilled and sliced straight from the can, on toasted brioche. It can also make a superb steak butter.

3 Pork rillettes This rich, creamy French pâté is usually made from belly pork, which is poached gently in its own fat, shredded and then returned to the fat and allowed to set firm. Rillettes from southwest France is superb. Eat it on hot toast, or spread it on ham, to roll up inside crusty rolls with gherkins.

4 Biltong A traditional southern African product valued for its long shelf life, biltong consists of narrow strips of game that are massaged to produce juiciness, rubbed in salt and then sun-dried until leather dry; it may also be smoked. A snack food in its own right, biltong can also be used in cooking. Sliver it and drizzle with avocado oil as an antipasto, or grate it into sautéed potatoes.

5 Jerky Similar to biltong, jerky is meat that has been cut into strips and then sun- or fire-dried. It originated in Peru and became the classic trail food of the American west. Try grating or slicing it into cooked bean, potato and pasta dishes.

6 Pastrami Lean, crimson pastrami, popular in the United States, is beef brisket or underside that has been dry-cured with salt, sugar and spices, and then hot-smoked. Its dark edges and coarse texture make it easily identifiable. Serve it on rye bread, with mustard and dill pickles, or with coleslaw or sauerkraut.

7 Corned beef Also known as bully beef, canned corned beef is spicy, sweet and fat-speckled. Highly nutritious and calorific, it was popularised as a wartime food. It can be sliced and eaten straight on bread with mustard or pickles, or torn into shreds and mashed into beans or potatoes.

8 Smoked venison This product, often from Scotland, is prepared from succulent lean venison, and is usually sold presliced in convenient vac-packs. It is best served cold, in sandwiches, with lettuce and redcurrant jelly, mustard or even horseradish sauce.

9 Smoked duck breast Rosy or dark, with a delicious border of fat, smoked Muscovy duck breast is delicious served with chilli jam and crisp lettuce, or with apple sauce or redcurrant jelly as a sandwich. Alternatively, heat it briefly in meat stock and port, and serve with mashed beans and carrots.

10 Bresaola This northern Italian speciality (similar to Swiss Bündnerfleisch) is lean, prime beef that has been air-dried until fully matured. It keeps a superb dark red colour, as well as its sweetness. Served sliced, drizzled with olive oil, and seasoned with a squeeze of lemon juice and a twist of black

3

4

5

6

7

8

9

10

11

12

pepper, it is the perfect antipasto. Or wrap it around a pork roast.

11 Confit de canard Using an ancient preservation method, duck legs are cured (using sugar, salt and seasonings) and then cooked slowly in their own fat until very tender, usually in the same vessel that they are sold in. The fat sets solid as a seal, the meat suspended between the fat and the naturally developed aspic below.

Add confit to cooked flageolet beans for a quick cassoulet, or eat it torn into shreds, with mustard.

12 Lacquered duck Delicious, glossy, rich and flavourful, lacquered duck is best bought whole or halved from an authentic Chinese delicatessen or restaurant. Prepared by air-drying and curing in sugar, salt and star anise, it is coated many times in an aromatic sticky glaze. Eat it, shredded, with hoisin sauce and crisp greens, wrapped in a Chinese pancake, Peking duck-style. Or chop it and add it to vegetable or noodle soup, or to quick-cooked wheat noodle dishes.

storage
Most of the products featured should be stored in a cool larder, or the fridge. Refrigerate after opening, and use within several days.

chorizo and butter bean stew with garlic and thyme

This recipe, from the renowned Padstow chef-restaurateur's cookbook, *Rick Stein's Food Heroes*, is simplicity itself. It depends on large, plump butter beans and the spicy effects of good Spanish chorizo sausage. As Rick himself says: "I've always felt that the most important point about cooking good food is getting the best produce in the first place". If time is short, substitute two large jars of Spanish butter beans (labelled 'Judion de la Granja') instead of the dried type, adding them, drained, at the stage stated.

Serves 4

Ingredients
350g dried Judion butter beans, soaked overnight
225g hot chorizo for cooking, such as parrilla chorizo picante
50ml olive oil
5 garlic cloves, thinly sliced
½ medium onion, finely chopped
175ml red wine
400g canned chopped tomatoes
1 tbsp fresh thyme leaves
½ tsp salt
2 tbsp chopped fresh flat-leaf parsley

Method
1. Put the butter beans into a large pan with lots of water, bring to the boil and simmer for 1 hour or until tender. Drain and set aside.
2. Cut the chorizo into thin slices. Heat the olive oil and garlic in a pan over a medium-high heat until the garlic begins to sizzle. Add the chorizo and cook until the slices are lightly browned on either side, then add the onion and continue to cook until it has softened.
3. Pour in the red wine and cook until it has reduced to almost nothing. Add the tomatoes, thyme, butter beans and salt, and simmer for 15 minutes.
4. Scatter the parsley over, spoon the stew into deep, warmed bowls and serve with crusty fresh bread.

choucroûte

For this hearty Alsace dish, you can use all kinds of ready-cooked pork products, from black pudding to kasseler.

Serves 4 – 6

Ingredients
8 small waxy potatoes, peeled
1 small onion, finely sliced
300ml fragrant white wine, such as Riesling
1kg prepared sauerkraut
2 tbsp caraway seeds
1 tbsp juniper berries, crushed
2–2.5kg assorted cured pork, ham or bacon, or sausage chunks: 400–500g of each

Method
1. Put the potatoes, onion and half of the wine into a large flameproof casserole and cook for 10 minutes. Add the sauerkraut, caraway seeds and juniper berries, and then tuck in the chunks of meat. Drizzle over the remaining wine.
2. Cover and simmer for 20 minutes, then uncover and raise the heat. Check that the meats are heated through, and cut into smaller pieces so that there is a portion of each per serving. Return the meats to the pan and cook for 5 more minutes.
3. Serve the choucroûte in a large dish with rye bread and mustard, with some chilled Riesling.

duck confit with cannellini beans

One of the simplest and tastiest recipes ever, in which the beans balance the richness of the duck confit.

Serves 3–4

Ingredients
1.5kg jar or can of duck confit
2 garlic cloves, crushed
½–1 tsp sea salt, crushed
20 black peppercorns, crushed
1kg good-quality canned or bottled cannellini beans
chopped parsley

Method
1. Stand the jar or can of confit in hot water for 5 minutes, and then gently ease out the contents.
2. Pull or cut the duck confit into 3 or 4 equal portions and sizzle, skin down, in a dry pan for 5 minutes.
3. Measure about 150g of the fat and all the jelly from the confit jar into a large flameproof casserole. Add the garlic, salt and peppercorns, and then the duck portions.
4. Drain off and reserve the liquid from the beans, and tip them into the pan. Cover and cook over medium heat for 10–15 minutes. Pour in enough of the bean liquid to make a runnier sauce. Turn up the heat until the stew bubbles hard.
5. Mash some of the beans in the pan to a rough purée.
6. Serve each chunk of confit with some of the bean mixture and scatter with some parsley. Eat with really good bread and accompanied by a robust red wine.

fish and seafood in cans and jars

Sardines lined up on garlicky toast, matjes herrings and a warm potato salad, exotic smoked sturgeon in a crisp pastry case and unctuous anchoïade: these are just a few of the earthy pleasures that await us once we investigate the intriguing selection of fish and seafood preserved in cans and jars. Not only are these foods ready to eat, they are also easy to use, intensely flavourful and have a long shelf life. Expect to pay reasonable prices for canned fish — it is only as good as the fish that first went into the tin. Look for products preserved, ideally in good olive oil, not harsh tasting sauces or marinades, which are often used to hide the lack of flavour of poor-quality fish.

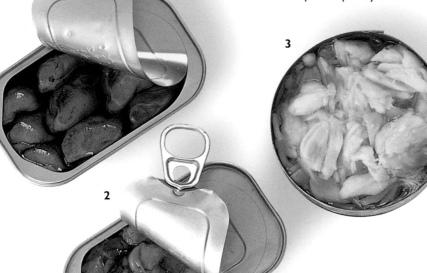

6 Snails These meaty creatures are often sold canned, with their shells in an adjacent pack. The large Burgundy snail and the smaller *petit-gris* are the best-known species. Ready-prepared for quick reheating, they are best baked in a 'snail butter' of garlic, butter, parsley, tarragon, onions, and sometimes Pernod. Alternatively, reheat them in a garlicky red wine sauce.

7 Pickled herrings (rollmops) Boneless, double herring fillets, rolled up in a vinegary marinade that sets the flesh dense and white, are known as rollmops. Use them in open sandwiches, with beetroot, onion or apple, or sliver and toss with white cabbage, onion, currants and mustard-dill dressing as a salad.

8 Matjes herrings in oil These lightly salted, marinated herring fillets are nutritious, tasty and a Jewish favourite. Traditionally served with steamed potatoes, gherkins and soured cream, they also taste good straight. Or cut the fillets into chunks and toss them with soft-boiled eggs, chives and thinned mayonnaise to eat with bread.

4 Prawns Large, plump king prawn tails keep good colour, texture and flavour when brined and bottled; the best ones often come from Scandinavia. The prawns are superb on toast with lemon mayonnaise and a sprinkle of chives and dill, and are useful in salads, too. Use both the liquid and the prawns in spicy seafood pilaus, fish soups or creamy prawn curries.

5 Clams These sweet, nutty and delicate bivalves are best canned in their shells (though often they are not). Use them in fish soup, with butter, garlic, onion and white fish, or in a sauce for spaghetti or rice: reduce the liquid to one-quarter of its volume, add onion, garlic and olive oil or cream, replace the clams and reheat. Or eat them straight, with sizzled pancetta, lemon juice and parsley.

1 Smoked mussels Shelled mussels, hot-smoked to fragile tenderness and sold packed in olive oil, are great eaten straight, or in rye bread sandwiches with onion and curried mayonnaise. Mashed up with butter, lemon juice, garlic and parsley, they make simple rillettes, and they excel in fritters, pancakes and salads.

2 Smoked oysters Salted and smoked oysters are intensely sea-flavoured and delicious. Drain, add lemon juice, and eat them plain or on cream cheese-covered toast or garlicky bruschetta with red onion and basil. Or wrap the oysters in pancetta and grill, add them to a rice salad, or mash them to a paste together with lemon juice, garlic, cayenne pepper and mascarpone.

3 Crab The best canned crab is white, dense and meaty. Mix the flesh into home-made mayonnaise, to be eaten with lemon and brown bread, or use it to stuff eggs; or toss the crab in garlicky vinaigrette and pile it on to lettuce. The canning liquid is good in sauces and soups.

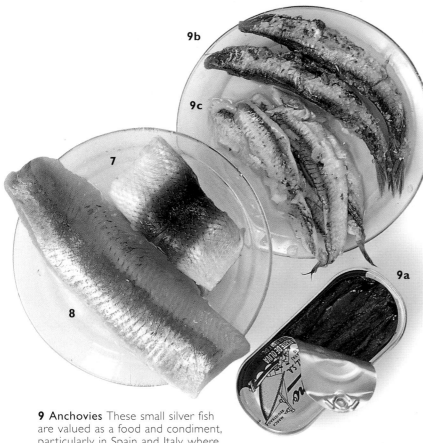

11 Mackerel en escabeche Fillets of horse mackerel, often Spanish, are canned using a chilli-hot tomato marinade that effectively 'cooks' the fish into dense flakes. Coarsely mashed with butter, a little marinade and parsley, it makes good rillettes, and it is also good in fish cakes or fish pie.

12 Tuna Various species of tuna are used for canning. The best, such as atún blanco, or white tuna (a), from Spain, has a satisfyingly meaty texture, and is relatively expensive. Yellowfin tuna (b), often Spanish, has a lighter meat and is also good quality. Always buy large steaks, packed in good olive oil, or water, rather than fragments.

Flake tuna into salads or into fillings for pitta, pancakes or rolls, or purée it for sauces (tuna suits olive- and tomato-based sauces). Tuna is also excellent with mayonnaise and vinaigrette, and capers, gherkins, garlic, herbs and lemon are all natural allies.

13 Sprats These small fish from the herring family, silvery gold from their hot dry-smoking, are delicious, but not widely available. Try grilling them briefly to serve with mustard or tomatoes on toast; add them to salads, or use them on pizzas instead of anchovies. Mashed up with lemon juice, butter and cayenne, they make a quick pâté.

14 Smoked sturgeon Not commonly available fresh, sturgeon is deliciously meaty when smoked. Dryish and easily flaked, it is good as a salad, in a lemony mayonnaise or a yoghurty vinaigrette. Puréed with butter, garlic and Pernod, it makes a good spread for toast.

9 Anchovies These small silver fish are valued as a food and condiment, particularly in Spain and Italy, where the best anchovies come from. They come salted and then canned, ideally, in olive oil (a), dry-salted (b) or marinated (c). Dry-salted and canned anchovies are the most useful, for boosting sauces, dressings, pastes and butters, and for enriching meat dishes. Marinated anchovies should be eaten raw: add them to salade niçoise, or serve them as part of a stylish appetiser.

10 Sardines Young pilchards, sardines are a humble but hugely successful canned fish. The best are from Spain, Portugal and France. Buy them whole and preserved in oil rather than in a marinade or sauce. Mashed together with butter, vinegar and mace, they are great on toast. Layered with apple, onion and cooked potato slices, they make a good main dish.

spaghetti with anchovy, tuna and caper sauce

This delicious recipe is storecupboard cooking at its easiest and best.
If the basics are of good quality, the result can be spectacularly delicious.

Serves 4

Ingredients
350g dried spaghetti
2 tbsp virgin olive oil
2 garlic cloves, slivered
6–8 anchovy fillets in oil, drained
250g canned white tuna in olive
   oil, drained
50ml white wine
75g capers, rinsed and drained
3 tomatoes, chopped
4 sun-dried tomatoes in oil,
   chopped
16 basil leaves
2 tbsp extra virgin olive oil
sea salt and freshly ground black
   pepper

Method
1. Cook the spaghetti in a large pan of boiling salted water for about
8 minutes or following pack instructions, until *al dente*.
2. Meanwhile, heat the first measure of olive oil in a frying pan, and
add the garlic. Sauté gently for 2–3 minutes.
3. Add the anchovy fillets and cook very gently until they reduce to
a mush. Increase the heat and stir in the tuna.
4. Heat the fish mixture for a few minutes, covered, then pour in the
wine and allow it to evaporate off and reduce. Stir in the capers,
tomatoes and sun-dried tomatoes.
5. Drain the pasta, reserving a little of the cooking water. Toss the
spaghetti and the sauce together in a warmed serving bowl. Add a little
of the cooking water if the sauce is too thick.
6. Stir in the basil leaves and the extra virgin olive oil and season to
taste. Serve hot, with some crusty bread and a lively white or red wine.

salt cod with chillies and garlic

This superb Basque dish is by American author and food expert Paula Wolfert, from her classic book *The Cooking of South West France*. In it, salt cod is simmered in garlic and olive oil until a rich, gelatinous emulsion forms. Chunky pieces of salt cod are best for this dish: you may have to buy more than you need, but you can use the off-cuts for brandade or for use with a garlicky aïoli dip.

Serves 4

Ingredients
500g boneless salt cod
250ml milk
4 tbsp olive oil
4 garlic cloves, peeled and
 thinly sliced
1 small chilli, cut into very
 thin strips
2 tbsp chopped fresh parsley

Method
1. Soak the cod in cold water for 18–24 hours, changing the water three times, and adding the milk during the last soaking.
2. Rinse the fish. Cut into 8 equal chunks. Remove the bones and scales but not the skin (which is needed for its enriching gelatinous quality). Set each piece on kitchen paper, on a plate. Chill for about 20 minutes.
3. Place the salt cod chunks, skin side down, in a 25cm round earthenware cooking dish or an enamelled cast-iron pan. Pour the olive oil over the fish and add the garlic. Put the dish over a low heat (a heat diffuser or trivet can prevent the dish from cracking).
4. Cook for 30 minutes, shaking the dish often so that the juices mix with the oil. Do not turn the fish, but shake and reposition the pieces to prevent sticking. Now and then, tilt the pan and spoon the simmering juices over the fish.
5. Near to serving time, increase the heat, and bring almost to boiling. Add the chilli and parsley; and cook to reduce the emulsifying juices somewhat, swirling constantly to combine the flavours. The result should be a smooth, blended sauce.
6. Serve hot, straight from the dish, or on individual serving dishes.

smoked salmon pizza

This pizza, invented by Wolfgang Puck, an influential chef-restaurateur and launcher of new trends in Californian cuisine, is lifted into the realms of luxury by the addition of smoked salmon.

Serves 2
(dough makes 4 x 20cm pizzas, topping covers 2 pizzas)

Ingredients

1 packet active dry yeast or
  ½ sachet fast-acting
  (micronised) yeast
1 tsp clear honey
375g plain flour
1 tsp kosher or rock salt
1 tbsp extra virgin olive oil

For the topping:
2 tbsp chilli and garlic oil
70g red onion, thinly sliced
4 tbsp dill cream (see below)
150g smoked salmon, thinly sliced
2 tsp chopped fresh chives
2 tsp sevruga caviar (optional)

Method

1. To make the dough, combine the yeast, honey and 55ml warm water in a bowl. In a mixer or food processor bowl, combine the flour and salt. Add the olive oil, the yeast mix and 175ml more warm water.
2. Mix on a low speed, or pulse, in bursts, until the mixture comes away from the sides of the bowl. Turn the dough out and knead for 2–5 minutes. Cover with plastic wrap and leave to rise in a warm place for 30 minutes. When it is ready, it will stretch when pulled.
3. Divide the dough into two; one half will keep for 2 days in the fridge or can be frozen. Divide the remaining dough into 2 balls. Shape each by pinching the sides underneath, curving the top surface. Do this several times. Then roll the dough under your palm repeatedly for about 1 minute until smooth, and firm. Rest it for 15–20 minutes.
4. Place 2 pizza stones or heavy metal baking trays in an oven, pre-heated to 240°C/Gas 9. On a lightly floured surface, stretch or roll out each piece of dough into a 20cm circle, making the outer edge a little thicker than the centre. Brush the dough with the oil and arrange the onions on top. Bake until the crust is golden brown (6–8 minutes).
5. Remove the pizzas from the oven and set on a firm surface. Spread the dill cream over the centre of each and then arrange slices of salmon to cover the pizzas. Sprinkle with chopped chives. If you like, spoon a little caviar on top and serve immediately.

to make dill cream

Mix 175ml soured cream with 1½ tablespoons minced shallots, 1 tablespoon chopped fresh dill, 2½ teaspoons fresh lemon juice and ⅛ teaspoon freshly ground white pepper. Mix well, refrigerate and use as needed. The dill cream should keep well for up to 1 week.

oils, fats
& milk
products

1   2   3   4   5   6

oils

In cooking terminology, oils are fats, derived from various plant sources, that are liquid at room temperature. Many of the oils on supermarket shelves are highly processed and often lacking in flavour. The best oils, obtained simply, without heat, such as cold-pressed extra virgin avocado oil, stay deliciously true to their origins. Over twice as calorific as proteins and carbohydrates, oils should be used with restraint. High in monounsaturated fatty acids, olive oil is the healthiest oil to use in large quantities, while most other common oils are high in polyunsaturated fat and are best used in moderation.

Some oils, such as argan and pumpkin seed oil, are pungent, while sunflower and grapeseed oil are bland. Nuts or seeds may be roasted prior to the extraction of oil, which produces a darker colour and stronger flavour. Flavoured oils, such as chilli or annatto oil, are useful, colourful and tasty, but 'aromatised' or herb-infused oils spoil quickly. Avoid anything labelled simply 'vegetable oil': good oils always designate their type and origins.

Oils must be stored in a cool, dark and dry place. Light and heat damage the molecular structure and will turn the oil rancid.

1 Sunflower oil This bland but nutritious oil is a workhorse oil for all purposes, and is not used for its taste. Use it in cakes, biscuits and breads, braised dishes and stir-fries, or for deep-frying and sautéing.

2 Groundnut oil (peanut oil) The groundnut, or peanut, contains about 50 per cent oil and is a good source of vitamin E. The oil has a distinctive taste, especially when the nuts have been roasted. This is an all-purpose oil, but it suits African and Asian dishes, and spicy food.

3 Grapeseed oil Pressed from the seeds left behind after wine-making, grapeseed oil is a light oil that is pleasant in most cooking, including in salads and cakes. It works well mixed 1:1 with extra virgin olive oil in mayonnaise.

4 Pumpkin seed oil This oil, which has long been popular in Central and Eastern Europe, has a wonderful, nutty flavour. Its colour varies from yellow to dark brown depending on whether the pumpkin seeds were roasted before pressing.

7   8   9   10   11   12

Drizzle it over white cheese salads, or on pasta, gnocchi, poached meats and vegetable purées.

5 Chilli oil The vivid red colour of this hot, chilli-flavoured oil is sometimes enhanced by food colouring. In Canton, it is used as a condiment in small side dishes. You can use it in Asian and Mexican cooking, for drizzling over fish, for example. Or try swirling it into toasted sesame oil as a 'dip' for crisp baby vegetables, with sea salt.

6 Sesame seed oil This is pressed either from unroasted seeds, which produces a fairly mild and pale oil, or from roasted seeds, which produces an oil as dark as mahogany with a rich, intense flavour. Sesame oil benefits Chinese and Indian dishes, often being added in small quantities at the end of cooking, or used as a condiment.

7 Hazelnut oil Known also as filbert oil, hazelnut oil may be pressed either from unroasted or roasted nuts. It is rich in vitamin E, distinctively nutty, and expensive.

Use it as a condiment to add nuttiness to cooked vegetables, chicken, fish and dressings. For sautéing, dilute it 1:2 with avocado or groundnut oil.

8 Walnut oil Produced mainly in France and Italy, walnut oil is expensive and can have a very strong taste that does not appeal to everyone. Use it in tiny amounts as a condiment with chicken and steamed greens, or in nut pastes, bean purées and vinaigrettes.

9 Palm oil (dende oil) An orangey red oil, often semi-solidified if cold, palm oil is produced from the fibrous fruit of the African oil palm. (Oil is also pressed from the inner kernels, but this is pale and more delicate.) It gives colour and characteristic earthiness to African dishes. Use it in peanutty stews, chicken sautés, fish curries and in pie fillings, but be warned that it is an acquired taste.

10 Mustard oil This yellow, spicy pungent oil gives an intense hotness to dishes and is important in India

and other parts of Asia. Note, however, that this oil contains erucic acid and is considered by some authorities to be toxic. If you choose to try it, use it in minimal amounts as a condiment, or for tempering spices for fish dishes.

11 Avocado oil Developed in New Zealand for culinary use, avocado oil is an excellent source of vitamin E. Look for the cold-pressed extra virgin variety in delis and the best supermarkets.

Avocado oil's high smoke point makes it good for frying, although it is most often used as a condiment: its greenish tones and fruity taste make it excellent with seafood, chicken and mozzarella, and also in stir-fries.

12 Moroccan argan oil Produced from the fruit of the Moroccan ironwood tree (which is similar to the olive tree but unrelated), this is the latest in gourmet oil discoveries, and therefore expensive. Use it in tagines and couscous, or with stuffed flatbreads and goat's cheese: it is distinctively pungent.

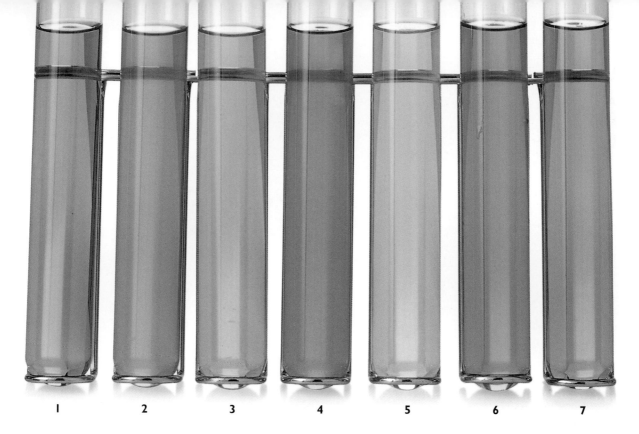

olive oil

Almost a 'pure fruit juice', olive oil is what is left once the olives have been pressed and the watery liquids removed. The best, least processed, olive oils retain all the fruits' natural anti-oxidants and vitamins, and have the best flavour.

Olive oil, produced mainly around the Mediterranean, is graded according to international standards. The different grades reflect, among other things, the degree of free acidity: the lower the free acidity, the smoother the taste. International brands often favour blends of different oils since this ensures greater consistency from year to year. When buying the best extra virgin olive oils, look for the country (or estate) of origin, the olive type, and the date and style of pressing. Be critical of the smell and taste: buy only those that you enjoy. In Italy, northern oils made from early-picked olives have greater pepperiness than southern oils made from late-picked olives.

1 Affiorato (flor de aceite) This superb 'flower of the oil' is as good as olive oil gets. Produced by crushing, before the main pressing begins, this free-run oil collects by gravity. It is made in France, Spain, Italy, Greece and even in New Zealand, but is very rare and therefore expensive. Use it as a condiment, drizzled over salads, or with garlic and salt on crusty bread.

2 First cold-pressed, extra virgin This prime and expensive product, which is obtained from the very first pressing, retains all the natural goodness of the olives, and has superb taste and smell.

Use it as for affiorato, for salads, dressings or bread-dipping, and some low-temperature cooking.

3 Extra virgin (supermarket grade) What's missing in this extra virgin oil – 'first' and 'cold-pressed' – is important, but many supermarkets commission consistent blends, which have a good colour, smell and taste, with no aggressive pepperiness and a fresh, fruity flavour. Perfect for everyday cooking, this oil can be used in all kinds of European dishes: to sauté, shallow fry, braise, stew, roast, or to use in mayonnaise, vinaigrettes, marinades and soups.

4 Unfiltered extra virgin Left unfiltered, extra virgin olive oil is cloudy and dense but tastes delicious. Olive oil that is lightly filtered (using cotton wool in a funnel) also tastes superb. Use either unfiltered or lightly filtered olive oil where full flavour counts: on bread, grilled vegetables, poultry, fish, pasta, rice or salads.

5 Virgin Obtained by one of the certified acceptable international methods of production, virgin olive oil is the second-best grade after extra virgin. While it may still have a respectable taste, this oil is best used for bulk cooking, deep-frying or mass consumption.

6 Feral Another rare and curious olive oil, this prime, usually blended, product from hand-harvested, wild (feral) trees, has unique appeal and earthiness. Use it as a condiment, for dipping bread into, or for pouring over cooked fish or meat, or steamed vegetables.

7 Truffle-flavoured Sold in tiny bottles, this expensive oil is made from extra virgin olive oil that has been flavoured with the aroma and taste of black or white truffles: the best also contains truffle pieces, musky and sulphurous. Use truffle oil late in cooking, with pasta, rice, mushrooms, foie gras and game.

using oil

Always match the oil to the style or origin of the dish. Oils with high smoke points, such as sunflower, groundnut and corn oils, are best for deep-frying. Virgin (but not extra virgin) olive oil is also a useful frying medium. Oil that has been heated over and again in a deep fryer will become rancid – it will keep longer if it is strained between frying and kept in a cool, dark place.

Vinaigrette

Put 1 tablespoon Dijon mustard into a jar or bowl. Add salt and pepper, some crushed garlic, and 2 tablespoons tarragon, cider or red wine vinegar. Shake or whisk well. Now add 6, 8 or 10 tablespoons extra virgin olive oil (that is, 3, 4 or 5 times the volume of the vinegar), according to your taste. Shake or whisk again until a dense, yellow emulsion forms.

Use this as a salad dressing, a sauce for vegetables or tomatoes, or as an accompaniment for steamed or baked fish, eggs or boiled meats. Store airtight, in a cool, dark place. Use within 2 weeks.

Note: Vinaigrette may separate: simply shake or whisk it, and magically it will emulsify once more.

Herb tempura

Wash and pat dry 16–20 bouncy sprigs flat-leaf parsley or wild rocket. Whisk together 1 egg yolk, 1 tablespoon water and 8 tablespoons fine rice flour. In another bowl, whisk 1 egg white together with a pinch of salt until frothy. Fold the two egg mixtures together.

In a medium pan, heat 5cm of peanut oil, virgin avocado oil, virgin olive oil, or a mixture of these to about 180°C, until a 1cm cube of bread browns in 30 seconds. Dip the herbs in the batter. Lower 3 or 4 sprigs gently into the hot oil and cook until pale, crisp and golden: just 1–2 minutes. Drain them on crumpled kitchen paper. Serve hot, as snacks, with a dipping sauce such as tamari or sweet chilli sauce.

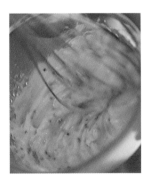

Mayonnaise

Put 1 egg yolk (it must be at room temperature), ½ teaspoon crushed sea salt flakes, ¼ teaspoon ground pepper, 1 chopped garlic clove (optional), about 1 tablespoon coarse-grain mustard, and 2 tablespoons lemon juice into a medium, high-sided bowl. Have ready an electric beater or balloon whisk. Mix together 125ml moderately flavourful extra virgin olive oil with 125ml grapeseed or peanut oil. Add this oil, in a gradual drizzle, using one hand, while whisking constantly with the other. The yolk-oil mixture will stiffen and then relax into a rich emulsion sauce that will keep its shape and gloss. Use, ideally within the day, as a sauce, dip, spread or accompaniment to soft-boiled eggs, salad leaves, sliced tomatoes or warm potatoes. With freshly cooked crab or lobster, this mayonnaise is celestial.

Note: Pregnant women, immune-damaged individuals, as well as the very young or elderly, should avoid eating real mayonnaise.

Marinating olives

Salt-cured olives can be mellowed, aromatised, plumped up and further preserved using heated extra-virgin olive oil as a marinade. Pack 250–300g dried black olives of choice into a heatproof, 500ml glass container. Sit it on a heatproof surface. Push in some sturdy fresh herbs, such as rosemary, bay and oregano, and add some spices, citrus zest and peppercorns. Heat 250–300ml extra virgin olive oil to 190°C, and pour it over the olives, just to overflowing, keeping your hands clear: it will splutter. The oil will actually 'cook' the olives. Leave to cool, cover and seal. Use the aromatised olives after 2 days, and they will keep for up to 2 months.

spaghetti with olive oil and garlic

One of the simplest, most perfect dishes ever: pasta dressed with garlicky, chilli-spiked olive oil. You can finish the dish off with fresh herbs and Parmesan, if you like, but all that really matters is the effect of the oil on the pasta. Use a first, cold-pressed extra virgin olive oil, if you can.

Serves 4

Ingredients
250g dried spaghetti
2 garlic cloves, slivered lengthways
5 tbsp extra virgin olive oil
½ –1 tsp dried red chilli flakes
sea salt flakes and freshly ground
  black pepper

Method
1. Cook the pasta in lots of boiling, salted water, according to the pack instructions or until *al dente*. Drain, reserving 2 tablespoons of the cooking water.
2. Heat 3 tablespoons of the olive oil in the still-hot, empty pan. Add the garlic and cook gently, but do not allow it to colour.
3. Stir in the chilli flakes, then the hot pasta and the reserved cooking liquid. Toss all together, adding sea salt and black pepper to taste.
4. Serve the pasta hot, with the remaining oil drizzled over the top.

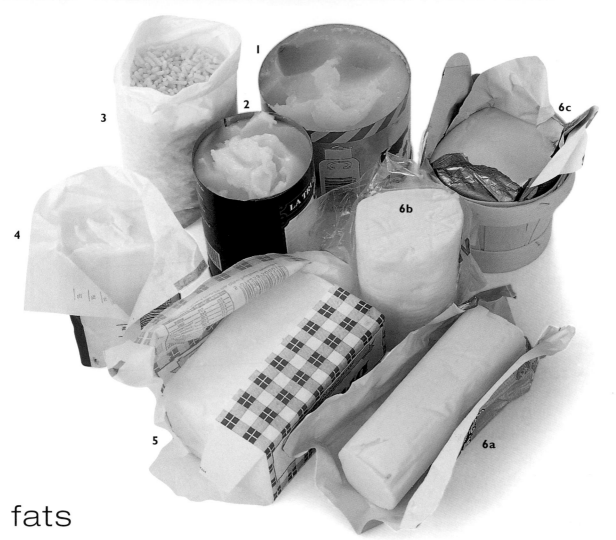

fats

Fats act as enrichers, they preserve, they help create flaky layers in pastries, they thicken watery liquids. They also taste good in their own right: butter, melted, is one of the simplest sauces ever. Dripping, lard and goose fat were once criticised for being 'saturated' fats, but now they are being re-evaluated as some of the most honourable, delicious and, perhaps, even heart-healthy foods. Even so, being rich, calorific and slow to digest, fats are best used in moderation.

Fats carry distinctive flavours of their own, but may also absorb those of adjacent foods: store them in a cool, dark place, ideally in opaque containers or wrappers. Sunlight damages fats, creating off-flavours over time.

1 Ghee This dense, clarified butter fat is made by heating cows' milk until some of the milk solids caramelise and the water evaporates off. It tastes uniquely toasty, it does not burn, and it has a long shelf life. Ghee distinguishes many Asian dishes, including breads, desserts and grain dishes, and is used in tempering Indian spices.

2 Goose fat This soft, creamy and fragrant fat is produced naturally by the rendering of goose carcasses. The best versions are usually from rural France. Use the fat in confits, pâtés and cassoulets, or for frying or roasting potatoes.

3 Shredded suet Machine-shredded beef (or mutton) kidney fat, suet adds flavour to doughs, batters, dumplings, cakes and puddings.

Traditional in sweet British mincemeat, suet also excels in steamed suet puddings.

4 Dripping This naturally tasty rendered fat from beef is creamy and full of flavour when made well. Use it when cooking beef casseroles, to grate into dumplings for stews, or to sauté potatoes.

5 Lard This white pork fat is superb combined with butter in shortcrust pastry, but is most useful as a frying medium. With a high smoke point, lard is great for sautéing pork or bacon for stews, or for deep-frying fritters. Good-quality lard can also be used to add flavour to pea or cabbage soups and some biscuits.

6 Butter Whether it's used for spreading or cooking, butter is only

as good as the cream from which it is made. There are two main types. Sweetcream butter (a), the most popular in Britain and the United States, is made by churning pasteurised cream, and may be salted or unsalted. Lactic butter (b), usually unsalted, is popular in continental Europe; it is made by adding a lactic culture to the cream before it is churned. With its mild acidity, lactic butter often has more flavour than sweetcream versions. Lactic butter is great served in slivers with blue cheeses, or melted over asparagus or green beans. French butters are usually excellent, and include AOC butters (c), of guaranteed quality. Eat these in slivers with charcuterie or steak.

Store butter away from other volatile substances: it easily absorbs other flavours.

steaks with truffle butter

Serves 4

For 4 griddled beef steaks, prepare the following: mix together 50g diced salted butter; 20g finely sliced preserved black truffle; 4 crushed garlic cloves; 2 tablespoons chopped fresh tarragon, parsley or chives; and 1 tablespoon fresh lemon juice. Using a fork, beat to a paste. Spread the mixture on oiled foil and roll up into a 10cm cylinder. Twist the ends tightly closed. Chill for 4 hours or fast-freeze for 30 minutes. Unwrap, cut into slices, and set 2 slices on each hot steak.

cupcakes with lavender butter cream icing

Makes enough for 12 small cakes

Grind 1 tablespoon fresh lavender buds, 1 teaspoon Campari bitters (or 3 drops red food colouring) and 6 sugar lumps, using a pestle and mortar or an electric spice grinder, to a mauve powder. Whisk this into 50g cubed, softened, unsalted butter. Using an electric beater, gradually incorporate 50g sifted icing sugar and 2 tablespoons hot water, heated stock syrup or hot lemon juice. Use to decorate 12 small cakes, adding extra lavender buds or blooms as optional decoration.

beurre blanc with poached salmon

Serves 4

Whisk 75g good-quality unsalted butter (cubed) in a bowl over warm water until creamy. In a saucepan, cook 1 chopped shallot, 60ml tarragon vinegar and 60ml Sauvignon Blanc together until reduced by half: to 4 tablespoons. Whisk this, along with 1 tablespoon thick cream, into the soft butter, until mousse-like. Season. Spoon this warm, creamy sauce over hot fish and serve without delay. (Most versions whip the butter into the reduction: this is the reverse.)

brandy butter with citrus segments in brandy snaps

Serves 4

Assemble 50g softened butter; 50g icing sugar; 4 tablespoons Cognac; juice and shredded zest of 1 orange; 4 brandy snap baskets; 4 clementines in Cointreau syrup and additional icing sugar for dusting (optional). Whisk together the butter, sugar, Cognac and some of the juice until light and pale. Add the remaining juice and most of the zest, to taste. Spoon some into each basket and add the clementine segments. Top with sifted icing sugar and orange zest, if liked. Serve within 2 hours.

milk products

While no cook doubts the deliciousness of cultured milk products, such as Greek yoghurt, nor should he or she rule out the benefits of canned or long-life milks, which can be used to make respectable dishes, from caramel custard to fish chowder. Coconut milk products are also perfect pantry foods: they have a long shelf life, and add instant richness to Asian foods.

Only milk products with a high butterfat content should be heated or boiled; these include clotted cream (55 per cent butterfat) and crème fraîche (35 per cent). Yoghurt with a butterfat content of 8–10 per cent curdles if boiled, so it should be stirred into hot foods just before serving. Coconut milk products should also be cooked gently, and never boiled.

1 Coconut cream Made from pressed grated coconut, and highly calorific, coconut cream can be used in Southeast Asian and Pacific cooking, especially curries, but also works well in Indian and African dishes, such as spicy stews, rice dishes and coconutty desserts.

2 UHT milk Long-life, or UHT (ultra-heat-treated) milk makes remarkably acceptable cheese sauce and chocolate pudding, and works well in cakes and other baked goods, too.

3 Coconut milk This is a thinner version of coconut cream and can be used in the same way.

4 Clotted cream This high-fat and dense, long-cooked cream is at its best when farm-produced in Devon or Cornwall, but it is mostly factory made. Use it dusted with sugar and grilled for a quick crème brûlée; eat it layered with berry fruits in

alcohol; or use it, with strawberry jam, to fill a sponge cake.

5 Crème fraîche This French 'fresh cream' is, in fact, a cultured product similar to soured cream. It needs no whipping and, being high in fat, is unlikely to curdle in cooked dishes (unless a low-fat version is used). It is delicious mixed with fresh fruit.

6 Greek yoghurt There is no substitute for this thick, full-cream yoghurt, which is curdled with bacteria and sometimes strained. Use it in dips and dressings, and in desserts – mixed with honey and pistachios, for example.

7 Creamed coconut Sold in a solid block, this is cheaper than coconut cream and keeps for longer once opened. You can make it into a coconut cream by melting it in milk or water, or else shave it directly into a dish towards the end of cooking. Use it in curries and kulfi.

8 Sweetened condensed milk This is milk that has been reduced by boiling to about one-third of its original volume. It consists of about 40 per cent sugar, and is great for making fudge. When simmered (unopened, in the tin) for two to three hours, it forms a dense caramel, which is superb in many Latin American, Asian and African desserts, tarts and ice creams.

9 Evaporated milk Reduced by evaporation to about half its original volume, evaporated milk is unsweetened. It is useful in sauces where reduction is needed, and in custards and rice puddings. Diluted with an equal quantity of water, it can replace fresh milk in cooking.

10 Dried full-fat milk Modern methods of drying mean that dried milk powders have a similar nutrient content to fresh. They are useful as a standby, for baking or sauces, and in Indian sweetmeats.

cheeses

Cheese has great significance in Europe and the Americas, less so in other parts of the world. At its best, cheese is a 'live' food which, thanks to helpful enzymes and micro-organisms, is in a state of continuous development. Thousands of cheeses exist, from very young, soft and mild cheeses to old, hard and pungent ones. The fat content varies from 1 to 75 per cent, but the protein levels are consistently high, making cheese an invaluable food and ingredient.

For the best cheese, find a retailer (or *affineur*) who keeps his or her cheeses in a cold, moist environment, allowing them to continue ageing naturally. Most cheese sold in the shops is stored in chill cabinets, which are too cold for the ageing process to continue.

1 Feta This creamy but crumbly, brine-ripened cheese from Greece is best made from mixed sheep's and goats' milk, but is now, alas, often made of cows' milk. Buy only Greek versions, which may be young (very soft), medium (firmer) or old (saltier, denser), and are best when *apo varelli* ('from the tub'). Dot feta over salads, or mash it to a paste with oil, garlic and mint.

2 Manchego Spain's most famous hard cheese, Manchego is made from sheep's milk and pressed into patterned moulds. It is sold either as fresh (*fresco*), slightly aged (*curado*), or older than three months (*viejo*). A full-fat cheese, with a creamy, firm interior, it is superb eaten with membrillo. Or try it sliced over roasted peppers or grated over vegetable soup.

3 Roquefort This noble French blue cheese, made from sheep's milk, is creamy, pungent and intense, but sweet, and with a silky mouth feel. It is superb both as a dessert, served with fresh berries, for example, and in cooking: mash it to a paste with Cognac and butter; slice and melt it over beef steaks; or add cream and melt it over piping-hot pasta.

4 Farmhouse Cheddar The world's most copied cows' milk cheese is epicurean when cloth-wrapped and farm-made, and usually acceptable when factory-made. A dense but flaky cheese, Cheddar is superb in many situations, but particularly grated into sauces, for cauliflower cheese, for example, and in soufflés.

5 Fromage frais This mild and soft, unripened cheese, with a fat content of 0–8 per cent, can be used like yoghurt, in cold desserts such as fools and ice creams, as well as in dressings: mixed with a little seasoning, vinegar and olive oil, it goes beautifully with watercress or chicory.

If adding fromage frais to a hot sauce, make sure you do it right at the end, to avoid curdling.

6 Crottin de Chavignol These small, fresh goats' milk cheeses from France are waxy with chalky centres and natural rinds, and shrink and become more pungent as they age. The cheese melts seductively when it is halved or sliced on to toast and grilled, or when shaved over hot rice, pasta or gnocchi.

7 Parmesan This superb, famous, flavourful and most typical Italian hard cheese, has its own denomination. In Italy the generic name for such cheeses is 'grana'; Parmesan – which is the abbreviated name of grana Parmigiano-Reggiano – is the best known version; grana Padano is another. Made of partly skimmed, unpasteurised cows' milk and matured for up to four years, grana has an intense fragrance and a flaky, grainy texture.

Buy small, rough-cut chunks to grate as needed, over risotto and pasta, or sliver and eat with Parma ham or other cured meats as part of an antipasto. Young Parmesan goes beautifully with ripe figs, peaches and pears.

8 Mozzarella This famously stretchy Italian whey cheese is made from cows' or, preferably, buffalos' milk. The curds are kneaded in whey until stretchy, and then hand-shaped into balls or plaits; these should always be sold packed in liquid. When really fresh, mozzarella tastes pleasantly milky and mild. (Beware porous, compressed blocks of so-called pizza mozzarella, usually

made outside Italy.) Traditionally sliced in a salad with tomatoes, basil and olive oil, or melted on pizza or in calzones, mozzarella also tastes great layered with avocado and anchovies on garlicky bruschetta.

9 Emmental This unpasteurised cows' milk cheese, with its distinctive holes, is Swiss in origin but now made elsewhere in Europe, often in France. It is creamy, with a rubbery texture and sweet, fruity taste.

Emmental is great to cook with. Better cubed than grated, it forms stretchy strands when heated, and is excellent in gratins, soufflés and fondues. Thinly sliced, it melts wonderfully over potatoes and gnocchi.

storage

Try to buy characterful cheeses little and often. Wrap them, loosely, in waxed or greaseproof paper rather than plastic, which causes cheese to sweat. Store cheeses in a cool, dark and well-ventilated place, isolated from other foods since they both absorb and transmit flavours, or in the fridge.

parmesan 'tuiles' with cheese cream
Makes 20. Serves 6

Divide 200g coarsely grated Parmesan cheese into 10g (or 1 tablespoon) piles. Arrange 4 of these on to one oiled baking tray. Bake in an oven preheated to 220°C/Gas 7 for 3½–5 minutes, until melted and golden. Use a palette knife to slide each hot tuile off the tray. Quickly lay them over the side of a small clean jar to cool. Repeat with the rest of the cheese. Once 20 are cooked, beat 100g Roquefort or Gorgonzola together with 50g cream cheese, 2 tablespoons fino sherry and 2 tablespoons chopped chives. Fill the tuiles with the mixture. Serve with chilled fino sherry.

twice-baked goat's cheese soufflés

Stephanie Alexander – a legendary Australian cook and author – gives us this marvellous recipe that uses goat's cheese in a very new way. The soufflés are not served in their dishes, so you can use any kind of mould, even teacups, as long as they have a capacity of about 150ml.

Serves 6

Ingredients
80g butter
60g plain flour
350ml warm milk
75g fresh goat's cheese
1 tbsp freshly grated Parmesan cheese
2 tbsp chopped fresh parsley
3 egg yolks
salt and freshly ground black pepper
4 egg whites
475ml cream

Method
1. Preheat the oven to 180°C/Gas 4. Melt 20g of the butter and use it to grease 6 soufflé dishes. Melt the remaining butter in a small, heavy-based saucepan. Stir in the flour and cook over a moderate heat, stirring for 2 minutes.
2. Gradually add the milk, stirring all the time. Bring to the boil, then reduce the heat and simmer for 5 minutes.
3. Mash the goat's cheese until soft and add it to the hot sauce, along with the Parmesan and parsley. Allow to cool for a few minutes. Fold in the yolks thoroughly and check the seasoning.
4. Beat the egg whites until creamy and fold quickly and lightly into the cheese mixture. Divide this between the prepared moulds and smooth the surface of each.
5. Stand the moulds in a baking dish lined with a tea towel and pour in boiling water to come two-thirds up their sides. Bake for about 20 minutes, until firm to the touch and well puffed.
6. Allow the soufflés to rest for a minute or so (they will deflate once out of the oven), then gently ease out of the moulds. Invert them on to a plate covered with cling film and leave until needed.
7. To serve, preheat the oven to 180°C/Gas 4. Place the soufflés in a buttered gratin dish so that they are not touching. Pour the cream over (about ⅓ cup per soufflé) to moisten them thoroughly. Return to the oven for 15 minutes. The soufflés will look swollen and golden. Serve with the cream from the dish or with fresh tomato sauce.

grains,
pulses & nuts

grains and meals

Grains, usually the seeds of grass-like plants, as well as their many derivatives, are among the world's most essential staple foods: imagine life without pancakes or porridge, baguettes or blinis. Whether we use them whole, cracked, rolled or popped, grain foods can create an inexhaustible range of superb dishes. Furthermore, they are perfect ingredients: they are compact, have a long shelf life, they transport easily, are affordable and adaptable, and are hugely nutritious. Included here, too, are meals, such as trahana and gari, which are not grains but are similar in their uses.

Dried grains are meant to keep, but they deteriorate over time. Use them within six months, before their natural oil turns rancid, a year at the most. Never mix a new batch with an old batch.

1

3

2

4a

4b

1 Barley couscous Less common than wheat couscous (see no. 5), these finely rolled grain fragments are treated in a similar way. Steam or sauté them and use them as a warm salad with garlic, aromatics and herbs.

2 Pearl barley While pot barley is barley which has some of its bran removed, pearl barley has almost no bran at all: so it cooks faster (in 60–90 minutes). Use it for vegetable soups, or Scottish cock-a-leekie soup, to which it adds a soothing gelatinous texture. Or cook it until tender in several times its volume of water, drain, and serve, dressed with yoghurt, mint and seasonings.

3 Pinhead oats When processed, oats produce oatmeal in various grades, from superfine (which cooks quickly and is a good thickener) to pinhead. The biggest and coarsest, pinhead oats cook slowly but make delicious porridge, and are good in

stuffings. Best known in cooler, northern regions, including Scotland and Ireland, pinhead oats produce a jelly-like softness once cooked.

4 Rolled oats These are made from dehusked oats (or groats), which are then steam-softened and rolled. Large jumbo oats (a) are often used in muesli. Smaller porridge oats (b), rolled pinhead oats, are quicker for making porridge than normal pinhead oats

(taking just five minutes to cook), but have less flavour; they are tastier if dry-toasted first.

Use rolled oat for flapjacks, or to coat filleted herrings or mackerel before frying in bacon fat.

5 Couscous Traditionally, this North African staple consists of coarsely ground hard wheat semolina, but most of what is available is a kind of granular semolina product, which has been precooked, and needs only to be steamed or left to stand in boiling water. Drizzled with butter or olive oil, and flavoured with spices, herbs, and perhaps harissa, couscous is superb served with lamb, fish or vegetable tagines.

6 Semolina Coarsely milled durum wheat, semolina, or finer semolina flour, are used to make pasta and gnocchi, though they are too hard to work into a dough at home unless combined with softer flours (see pages 136–7). But semolina can also be used (with sugar, vanilla and milk) to make sweet puddings or complex Indian sweets.

7 Ebly® wheat A relatively new 'designed' product, Ebly® wheat is durum wheat made tender enough to be cooked like rice. Interesting, chewy and adaptable, it can be cooked straight, in boiling water, or as for risotto (see page 108). Add butter, olive oil or cream, and then serve it with chicken, fish, tofu or precooked ham or bacon.

8 Trahana This large-crumbed grain product is popular in Greece and Turkey, but is used in some form in other countries, too. It is made from crushed wheat or flour, which is mixed with yoghurt and then left to sour before being air- or sun-dried. Trahana should be rehydrated in boiling stock, water or milk. Use it in soups, pilaus and stews, seasoned using tomato-based sauces, garlic or fresh herbs, and dampened with olive oil or butter. Or, add honey and nuts and serve it as a dessert.

9 Bulgur wheat Adaptable, easy to use, and tasty, this nutty cereal product (known also as burghul or cracked wheat) is used widely in Europe and the Middle East. Consisting of wheat grain that has been parboiled, dried and then 'cracked', it can be either boiled briefly in seasoned liquid or simply left to stand while the boiling liquid is absorbed. The grains readily absorb lemon juice and olive oil, too. The basis of tabbouleh, bulgur wheat is also useful in stuffings and kibbeh.

10 Hominy grits These dried and hulled maize kernels, high in fibre, are popular in the southern United States. They are most commonly eaten ground, as grits, as a savoury breakfast 'mash' with bacon and eggs. They can also be used, like other ground cereals, in bread and puddings.

11 Cornmeal This maize meal, naturally golden (pictured), blue or white, is an important staple in the Mediterranean, parts of the United States and the Caribbean. American cornmeal is finely ground and is perfect for making muffins and cakes. Polenta, the northern Italian staple, is coarsely ground cornmeal; it becomes creamy when boiled in water, but sets hard when cooled, and can be grilled, baked or fried.

Fine and coarse cornmeals can both be used in breads, cakes and batters, but the texture of the end product will vary according to the coarseness of the meal.

12 Buckwheat Nutty, angular buckwheat seeds are not a grain, in fact (they are related to rhubarb), but are regarded as a 'pseudo-cereal'.

Associated traditionally with Eastern Europe, buckwheat is used to make *kasha*, a Russian porridge-like dish that is served, habitually, with wild mushrooms and soured cream. Cooked in sweet stock, and with cherries, Kirsch and whipped cream stirred in, buckwheat makes a delicious dessert.

Buckwheat is also ground into flour (see page 136).

13 Gari Dried cassava meal rather than a grain, gari is granular and starchy, so is not dissimilar to a cereal. It is much loved in Brazil (where it is known as *farinha de mandioca*) and the West Indies. Boiled, gari makes a kind of meal porridge, which can be served with stews. In Brazil, *farinha de mandioca* is sautéed in bacon fat, butter or palm oil, and then sprinkled over cooked foods before serving.

5

10

6

11

7

12

8

13

9

storage
Minimally processed grains may sometimes harbour moths. Microwave such grains briefly in batches, cool, and transfer to airtight storage containers. Keep in a cool, dark place.

cooking rice

Everyone has their favourite way to cook rice. The basic method for cooking any kind of rice is in a large amount of boiling salted water, but each type of rice has its own traditional method. Some cooks advocate rinsing rice, to remove any surface starch (which can cause the grains to clump) but this is not necessary with most mass-produced rice. Soaking rice can reduce the cooking time, and help the grains to keep their shape, but for most types of rice this is strictly optional.

Cooking basmati rice
The simplest way to cook basmati rice is by the 2:1 absorption method. Put the rice, in cupfuls, in the pan (with spices, if you like) and pour in twice as many cupfuls of boiling water. Bring to the boil, cover, turn down the heat as low as possible and cook for 10–12 minutes, without stirring, until all the water has been absorbed, and the rice is tender.

Cooking paella rice
Although paella rice is short-grained, like risotto rice, it is cooked differently. After coating the rice in hot fat in the pan, you simply pour in boiling water (or stock) to cover generously. Keep extra boiling water on hand, which you can add if the rice looks dry. Use a spatula to check that the rice isn't sticking, but don't stir it. Add saffron towards the end, before adding other ingredients.

Cooking risotto rice
Once you have fried the onions and any other key ingredients in oil or butter, add the rice and fry it for a minute or so in the oil, which will help keep the grains separate. Add wine, for extra flavour, and when that has evaporated off, add hot stock by the ladleful, waiting for the liquid to absorb before adding the next one, until the rice is tender. This should take 20–30 minutes.

Making rice pudding
The stubby grains of pudding rice are transformed into a creamy, sticky mellowness when cooked slowly in vanilla-infused, sweetened milk. Follow the simple recipe on page 111. It may seem impossible that such a small amount of rice can thicken so much milk, but it does. And any milk that is still liquid solidifies once the pudding is cold, when it is equally delicious.

lionhead rice-pork balls
Serves 4

Microwave 225g black glutinous rice with 400ml boiling water, covered, on High for 20 minutes, until parcooked. Drain, reserving 100ml of the water. Mix one-third of the rice with 250g food-processed bacon and chicken mixture, adding 1 tablespoon rice flour, 2 teaspoons garlic purée, 4 tablespoons grated onion, 50g chopped broccoli, and 2 tablespoons chicken stock, Process again. Shape into 24 balls. Wet and coat each in a second third of the rice. Microwave, covered, for 20 minutes, until the rice coating is tender and the balls firm. Boil the reserved cooking water with some rice vinegar, five-spice seasoning, sugar and soy to make a dipping sauce, and serve with the remaining rice.

spanish rice with seafood
Serves 4

Sauté 350g Spanish paella rice in a wide shallow pan with 4 tablespoons olive oil, 4 sliced garlic cloves, 2 onions and some sea salt. After 3 minutes, stir in 1 litre fish stock. Cook over medium heat for 15–18 minutes, then add 12 raw prawn tails, 24 small clams, a handful chopped green beans and a pinch crushed saffron threads or $\frac{1}{8}$ teaspoon powdered saffron. Cook for 4 minutes more, until the rice is tender, turning the seafood at intervals. Add lemon juice and serve hot.

risotto with pesto
Serves 4

In a large shallow pan, heat 75g butter with 1 chopped onion and 2 chopped garlic cloves. Stir in 250g risotto rice. Add 100ml dry white vermouth: let it bubble off and evaporate. Ladle in 250ml hot chicken stock. Cook over medium heat for 18 minutes, adding more hot stock at roughly 6-minute intervals. Season using 100g fresh pesto. Cook for 5–8 minutes longer, until soupy and tender. Serve with Parmesan, some fresh basil and freshly ground black pepper.

vanilla rice pudding
Serves 4

Boil 600ml single cream with 400ml milk and pour over 2 sugar lumps with vanilla seeds (see page 16), the split vanilla pod itself, 75g pudding rice and 75g sugar in a large heatproof baking dish. Stir well. Bake, uncovered, for 3–4 hours at 170°C/Gas 3. Alternatively, microwave on High for 15 minutes (covered), stir, reduce the power to Medium and cook (covered) for a further 25 minutes. Either way, the liquid should be creamy and the rice soft. Sprinkle 25g muscovado sugar on top and grill (or blow torch) until golden and crusty. Serve hot, with cream.

handkerchief sushi

You can make these pretty, unconventional sushi shapes by using a twist of clean muslin or cling film, and your preferred flavourings and decorations. Heresy it may seem, but, if no Japanese sushi rice can be found, pudding rice is a passable imitation; it will just need extra liquid.

Serves 4 as a starter

Ingredients
1 tsp dashi stock granules
175g Japanese sushi rice, soaked, rinsed, drained
1 tsp puréed garlic
1 tsp puréed ginger
2 tbsp mirin
4 tsp rice vinegar

Fillings
6 umeboshi plums, quartered (or 4 tbsp umeboshi paste), or 50g canned clams, crab, smoked mackerel or salmon, drained, or 50g miso or bean paste

Garnishes
Choose from: nori seaweed; cured salmon or trout roe; strips of chives or spring onions; strips or slices of red or green chillies; tiny parsley or chervil sprigs

Method
1. Dissolve the stock granules in 200ml boiling water (or make dashi stock by traditional methods).
2. Add the rice to the stock in a pan, and bring to the boil.
3. Reduce the heat to maintain a simmer, cover and cook undisturbed for 10–12 minutes, until the liquid is absorbed and the rice is tender and sticky.
4. Add the next 4 ingredients, stir, then tip the seasoned rice out on to a tray. Fan it until cool enough to handle.
5. Divide the rice into 16–24 balls. Using clean hands, pick up one rice ball, push some filling deep inside, then close it.
6. Create a garnish on the opposite side of the ball. Roll the ball up in cloth or cling film, twisting it tightly underneath. Continue until all are made, then unwrap.
7. Serve the sushi with pickled ginger, mixed or ready-made wasabi, and tamari (Japanese soy sauce). Eat using chopsticks or your fingers.

bacon, barley and wheat chowder

Barley and wheat grains give this substantial soup-cum-stew its pleasant texture and body. Although Ebly® wheat is normally a rapidly cooked, 'instant' grain, in this recipe it is cooked slowly to add richness. With the bacon and other vegetables, this dish becomes a well-balanced meal-in-a-bowl.

Serves 4–6

Ingredients
750g rolled, smoked bacon joint
1 bay leaf, fresh or dried
1 handful fresh thyme
2 onions, halved
50g each pot barley, pearl barley
   and Ebly® wheat grains
8 small potatoes, peeled
6 sticks celery, quartered
1 sweet potato, peeled
1 ham stock cube, crumbled
single cream or milk
50g butter
50g plain flour
340g canned sweetcorn, drained
salt and freshly ground black
   pepper

Method
1. In a large saucepan, put the bacon with the bay leaf, thyme and onions and 1.5 litres water. Bring to the boil, reduce the heat, and simmer for 45 minutes, partly covered.
2. Add the barley and wheat grains, the potatoes, celery, and sweet potato. Poach for 45 minutes longer.
3. Pour off the liquid, reserving 600–750ml of it. Add the stock cube to the reserved liquid, and add enough single cream or milk to make up to 1 litre.
4. In a second saucepan, melt the butter. Stir in the flour, then whisk in the liquid, stirring, to make a creamy sauce.
5. Remove the sweet potato and the bacon and cut them into manageable chunks. Return these to the pan, along with the sweetcorn.
6. Add the creamy sauce to the pan. Season to taste with salt (if necessary) and black pepper. Reheat and serve the chowder hot in large bowls, with herbs and seasonings as liked.

pulses

Pulses, or the seeds of legumes, such as peas, beans and lentils, are delicious and have been a staple for millennia. Used whole, split, husked, cracked or ground, pulses dry and store well and are high in protein. Dried beans, which must usually be soaked before cooking, have the best taste and texture, but good-quality precooked, canned beans are useful when time is short. Dried beans must be boiled hard for ten minutes at the start of cooking, to inactivate potentially lethal toxins.

1a 1b 1c 1d

1e 1f 1g 1h

2 3 4 5

6

1 Haricot beans The dried beans of the *Phaseolus vulgaris* species, native to Central America, are known as haricot beans and are the most common pulses used in the West. Many varieties exist, which vary subtly in taste and texture but can be treated in similar ways, and are all available dry or canned. If dry, they require soaking then cooking for 30–60 minutes.

Glossy **red kidney beans** (a), famously used in chilli con carne and feijoada, go well with chilli and garlic. They can be blended in stock to make soup, mixed with rice, or added whole to casseroles. **Black beans** (b) are popular in Brazil and Mexico, especially in stews, and have a strong and meaty taste. Italians prefer pink, speckly **borlotti beans** (c) and white **cannellini beans** (d) for soups and stews.

Pale green **flageolet beans** (e) are prized in France: they go well

with lamb, whose juices they absorb beautifully. Small white beans known in Britain as **haricot beans** (f) hold their shape well and cook to a lovely creamy consistency; use them in soups and stews, with roasts, or casseroled with ham. The same beans are doused in tomato sauce and sold as **baked beans** (g), which are eaten on toast in millions of British households. **Pinto beans** (h), loved in Mexico and Spain, are good for mashed 'refried' beans, and can be bought canned in chilli sauce.

2 Butter beans (fava, judia) These large, white, kidney-shaped beans are popular all around the Mediterranean. After soaking, they should be cooked for about an hour. They are excellent with sausage, including chorizo, herbs and fresh tomatoes. Giant butter beans, called *gigantes*, are prized in Greece, and are now available in cans. Serve them either

heated up or cold with lamb or chicken, or as a salad.

3 Ful medames North African beans, very popular in Egypt, ful medames usually need cooking for up to two hours if bought dry. Add spices, olive oil and herbs (such as mint or parsley) to the beans towards the end of cooking, and serve them with flatbreads. Mashed to a paste, ful medames can be pushed inside pitta pockets along with crunchy pickles: a quick meal if you buy the canned type (pictured).

7   8   9   10

11   12   13a   13b

4 Black-eyed beans These creamy beans with black 'eyes', a variety of cowpea, are greatly loved in India, Mexico, the Caribbean and the United States, where they feature in Creole dishes. Nutty tasting, they go well with coconut, chilli, coriander and pork, and also make superb savoury bean cakes.

5 Aduki beans In China and Japan, these small, mild-tasting beans are often used as a sweet filling for steamed buns or dumplings. They are good mixed with other beans and aromatics, and with rice. Or add them to salads, casseroles, soups or noodle dishes.

6 Chickpeas These pulses are vital to Spanish, Latin American, Middle Eastern and Indian cooking. Dried chickpeas (pictured) are best used in spicy stews, but tinned chickpeas are more convenient for mashing to a creamy purée to mix with tahini, olive oil, garlic and lemon juice for hummus. Dried chickpeas, soaked, but not cooked, and ground up with herbs, spices and garlic, make falafel.

7 Green lentils These split lentils are the basis of millions of 'dal-roti' (lentils and bread) meals all over Asia. You do not need to soak them, but you can halve the cooking time, to 20 minutes, if you do. Good

with garlic, chillies and bay leaves, green lentils cook to a semi-soft mush, perfect for a soup or stew.

8 Umbrian lentils These brownish lentils from Umbria, in Italy, are delicious cooked (unsoaked) for 20–30 minutes with onion, garlic, celery and herbs, and served with bread, rice or pasta. Add strong meat essence, butter or olive oil and balsamic vinegar before serving.

9 Puy lentils These highly regarded French lentils can be cooked, unsoaked, in 15–20 minutes, and are deliciously nutty. They suit garlic, herbs and olive oil, and taste good with meat essence, duck or goose fat, or garlicky vinaigrette, especially one based on balsamic or sherry vinegar. Serve as a salad or accompaniment.

10 Yellow split peas Used world-wide in dhals, stews, soups and fritters, in Europe these peas are often turned into soups (with ham or bacon). Needing no soaking, they cook quickly to a mush. Ground dry to a powder, they act as an instant thickener.

11 Split red lentils Grown world-wide, split red lentils are known under many different names, including *masoor dal*. They are loved

for their cheerful colour, mellow taste, 20-minute cooking time and ability to absorb flavours. Use them in spicy stews, vegetable curries, dhals and soups; added in small amounts, they act as a thickener.

12 Black gram (urad) This valuable pulse is used with great ingenuity in India, either whole, split, or skinned. Split black gram (pictured), called *urad dal chilka* in India, is famous as the basis of many purées, which are known, confusingly, as dal, or dhal. It needs no soaking, but requires longer cooking than most small pulses. Small amounts of whole black gram, tempered in hot oil and spices, can be used as a seasoning to pour over rice.

13 Mung beans (green gram) Dried mung beans, popular all over Asia, are sold whole, split (a), in which case they are called *moong dal chilka*, or skinned (b), as *moong dal*. The beans should be soaked for two hours and then cooked for 15–20 minutes. Use them with salty-sweet or spicy accompaniments, in Asian-style rice dishes or in dumplings, ground up with spices, garlic and yoghurt.

14 Tofu (bean curd) Best-known under its Chinese name, tofu, this soya bean 'cheese' is soft, high in protein and low in calories, but also low in taste, which means that it needs assertive seasoning. Fresh tofu (a), which is best marinated before cooking, is good with garlic, ginger, soy and black bean flavours. Use it instead of egg or cheese to add a protein boost to vegetable, rice and noodle dishes. Silken tofu (b) has a longer shelf life (it keeps, unopened, for a year or so), is softer, and goes well in Asian-style soups, purées and sauces. Try it with fruit, in blended smoothie drinks.

14a   14b

lamb dhansak

Lentils are a staple of Indian cooking, and in this delicious recipe the talented Indian author, Monisha Bharadwaj, uses them with lamb, spices and seeds in an authentic Parsee dish.

Serves 4

Ingredients

300g lamb, trimmed and cubed
150g split yellow lentils
150g tomatoes, chopped
150g bottle gourd or butternut
  squash, chopped
2 large onions, finely chopped
6 tbsp chopped coriander leaves
6 tbsp chopped mint leaves
5 tbsp chopped red pumpkin
4 tbsp chopped fresh fenugreek
  leaves
1 tsp turmeric powder
1 tsp chilli powder
1 tsp sugar
salt
4 tbsp distilled vinegar
1 tbsp sunflower oil
1 tsp cumin seeds

Method

1. Put all the ingredients listed from lamb to salt in a heavy-based saucepan with 450ml water, and cook until the lamb is tender and the lentils are soft, 30–40 minutes.
2. Mash the vegetables and lentils with a wooden spoon, taking care not to break the meat. Add the vinegar and stir.
3. Heat the oil in a frying pan and fry the cumin seeds. Pour them over the curry.
4. Simmer for 5 minutes and serve the curry hot, with rice or Indian breads.

lentil chermoula soup with garlic scallops

This superb soup recipe from Paul Gayler, the prestigious executive chef at London's Lanesborough Hotel, shows off Puy lentils at their best. This is a hearty soup with fragrant Moroccan spices, topped with buttered, garlicky scallops. Prawns could replace the scallops, if preferred.

Serves 4

Ingredients

For the soup
4 tbsp olive oil
1 small onion, chopped
1 garlic clove, crushed
2.5cm piece root ginger, peeled
   and finely chopped
½ tsp ground cumin
½ tsp ground coriander
1 small red pepper, deseeded and
   chopped
3 ripe plum tomatoes, chopped
1 tsp harissa paste
200g Puy lentils, rinsed and drained
1 litre chicken stock
salt and freshly ground black
   pepper

For the garlic scallops
1 garlic clove, crushed
⅛ tsp dried chilli flakes
2 tbsp chopped fresh coriander
   leaves
8 fresh, juicy, large scallops,
   roe removed
2 tbsp olive oil

Method

1. Heat the olive oil in a pan, add the onion, garlic and ginger, and cook for 3–4 minutes until softened. Add the cumin and coriander. Cook for a further 2 minutes. Add the chopped pepper, tomatoes and the harissa. Cook over gentle heat until the vegetables soften.
2. Add the lentils and stock and bring to the boil, reduce the heat and cook until all the ingredients are tender, 30–40 minutes. Transfer to a blender and blitz to a smooth purée; season to taste.
3. For the garlic scallops, mix the garlic, chilli flakes and half the coriander in a bowl, add the scallops, mix together well and marinate for 1 hour.
4. To serve, heat the olive oil in a frying pan until smoking, add the scallops and cook for 1 minute on each side until golden and crusty on the exterior. Remove from the pan.
5. Pour the soup into 4 shallow serving bowls. Top each serving with 2 scallops, scatter over the remaining coriander and serve.

seeds and nuts

All nuts and seeds indicate potential future growth, and come packed with many essential nutrients. They are high in protein (and also calories) and contain valuable oils and fat-soluble vitamins. In Southeast Asia, India, Africa and the Middle East, nuts and seeds are combined with grains, breads and cereals to produce an amazing assortment of high-protein dishes. And imagine Italy without pesto, the United States without peanut butter, Austria without poppy seeds.

Whenever possible, buy nuts and seeds whole, in their shells: removing the shell at the time of use ensures maximum texture and flavour. The nutty flavour of some seeds and nuts, such as sesame seeds or pine nuts, improves if they are fried or dry-toasted. Store them in a cool, dark, dry place in order to prevent their fats from turning rancid and bitter.

1 Pumpkin seeds Inedible pumpkin kernels contain tender seeds. Often toasted with oil and salt as snacks, these are also delicious added to salads, pasta or noodles. Include them with a mix of grains in risotto, or use them with mashed beans or peas for spicy fritters or beancakes.

2 Sunflower seeds The seeds of the glorious sunflower, once dried and shelled, have a pleasant creamy texture and taste. They can be used raw in salads, scattered into noodles, or sizzled in virgin oil and poured over rice dishes.

3 Sesame seeds These tiny, oil-rich seeds are popular in Asian cooking as a coating or garnish, and in Europe as a topping for biscuits and breads. White sesame seeds (a) are immensely important and underpin many recipes, while black sesame seeds (b) have a slightly stronger, nutty, earthy flavour and are more of a curiosity. In the Indian sub-continent, they are often tempered

in hot oil and poured over grains or pulses before serving.

4 Poppy seeds Derived from the opium poppy, but not an opiate, black poppy seeds (a) have a nutty-sweet taste. Popular in Europe as a garnish, topping or filling, they often taste best if dry-toasted. Use them on white bread, to coat white fish-balls, or in cakes and pastries. Rarer white poppy seeds (b), used in Asia and the Middle East, are scattered over flatbreads or ground and used as a thickener.

5 Walnuts In many cultures, this delicious, slightly astringent nut is prized when green (for pickling), but is more commonly eaten ripe. Plain, walnuts are superb eaten with strong Cheddar and port. Ground up, they can be used as a thickener in Circassian chicken, or in biscuits.

6 Brazil nuts These rich and oily nuts from South America, if ground, make a moist meal that works well

in some cakes. Whole, they are good coated in chocolate or toffee, but are most useful chopped – to add to fudge, spice loaves or even curries or lentil patties. Brazils can also add crunch to fresh tomato, chilli and mint salsa for fish.

7 Cashew nuts These unusual and expensive nuts grow suspended beneath a red pear-shaped fruit and are never sold in the shell. Use them, plain or salted, in spicy, soy-flavoured chicken dishes and Indian stir-fries. Chopped into spicy fruit and nut mixtures to fill pastries, they provide a creamy texture.

8 Pecan nuts Related to walnuts, but with a more streamlined shape and a sweeter taste, pecan nuts can be used in all the ways that walnuts are. They work well salted and roasted in muffins and biscuits, or on cakes, and are the key ingredient in American pecan pie. They are also great in ice cream sundaes with maple syrup.

9 Pine nuts (pine kernels) These dense, creamy, oil-rich nuts, with a delicate resiny flavour, are the essential Mediterranean nut. Included most famously in pesto, they are also used in Italian cookies, nougat (*torrone*) and toffees. Pine nuts also add pleasurable 'bite' to rice dishes.

10 Hazelnuts (filberts, cobnuts) Usually sold shelled, without their brown skins, white, tender hazelnuts are useful in both sweet and savoury recipes. Try grinding them to mix with melted dark chocolate and cream for a spread, or use them whole in muesli, biscuits, muffins and cakes. Toasted, they are delicious scattered over noodles and rice.

11 Peanuts (groundnuts, monkey nuts) Technically, the peanut is not a nut: its parent plant is, in fact, a legume, the nuts being the peas in the pod. Sold unshelled or shelled (pictured), plain or roasted, peanuts can be ground and turned into home-made peanut butter, or used in satay and other Indonesian dishes, as well as in African chicken stews and fish curries.

12 Pistachios Grown in Greece and the Middle East, pistachios are popular worldwide. They are best bought in their tough shells (a), which can be prized apart to reveal the pink-skinned nut (b). The skin, in turn, can be removed by blanching, to reveal the luminously yellow-green flesh (c).

Add pistachios to chocolate, fudge, halva or Turkish delight, or try them in savoury dishes, such as terrines, or scatter them over white fish, for example. They are also superb puréed in ice cream.

13 Almonds These are an ancient Mediterranean food prized for their versatility, protein content and their white, creamy interior; Jordan almonds are the most highly regarded variety.

Almonds are crucial to Greek baklava and Italian amaretti, as well as to English Bakewell tart. They are also used in savoury dishes; they are popularly combined with trout, and with chicken or pork in China.

9 10 11

12a 12b 12c

For use in cooking, whole almonds (a) often have their brown skins removed, in which case they are known as blanched almonds (b). The white nut can then be sliced lengthwise, for flaked almonds (c), or cut across the width to give nibbed almonds (d). Finest size of all are ground almonds (e).

14 Macadamia nuts Native to Australia, the buttery-mild, waxy macadamia is among the most costly and rich of nuts. Macadamias can be used in stuffings, pushed whole into meat balls, chopped into cakes, biscuits or pastries, and added to sweet fillings or chocolate truffles. They also work beautifully in home-made dukkah spice mix (see page 13).

15 Chestnuts Lean, low in starch and high in protein, chestnuts grow best in Spain, Italy and France. They are sometimes available dried (a), suitable for grinding to a meal to give a protein and flavour boost to breads or cakes. But chestnuts are most easily bought whole and shelled, either vac-packed or canned (b); these can be used, chopped, in stuffing, or mixed with buttery potatoes and garlic, as a mash. Chestnuts can also be bought in the form of a purée.

13a

13b

13c

13e

13d

chopping nuts and seeds

When chopping nuts or seeds, do it by hand, using a cook's knife, in repeated motions, or a mezzaluna, in a rocking motion. Alternatively, use an electric spice grinder, but only in short bursts: too much and the nuts or seeds will be reduced to an oily paste. Leaving some chunkier pieces in the ground mixture can often improve the look, texture and mouth feel.

14

15a

15b

seeded bread

This bread is easy to make and has a delicious texture.

Makes 2 small cobs

Ingredients

500g plain flour or strong white bread flour

1 × 7g sachet micronised yeast (fast-acting, powdered yeast)

2 tbsp soft brown sugar

2 tsp sea salt flakes

3 tbsp extra virgin olive oil

50g each of sesame seeds, blue poppy seeds, sunflower seeds and pumpkin seeds (dehusked)

2 tbsp malt extract, or golden syrup

4 tbsp honey mixed with 2 tbsp hot water, to glaze

Method

1. Put the flour, yeast, sugar, and salt in a bowl, and stir with a fork until they are well mixed. Add 300ml warm water and just under 2 tablespoons of the olive oil. Mix until the dough clings together.
2. Gather the dough into a ball and tip it out on to a lightly floured work surface, and knead for 2 minutes.
3. Rub a large bowl with a little oil, and put in the dough, turning it over to coat it with the oil. Cover with a plastic bag and leave to rise, in a warm place, for 1 hour, or until the dough doubles in bulk.
4. Punch the dough down. Turn it over and reshape it into a ball. Divide this into two.
5. Combine the seeds, and mix them with the remaining olive oil and the malt extract or golden syrup; divide into two. Pat out each ball of dough and fold the nut mixture evenly through both.
6. Shape the dough into 2 rounded loaves, put on a well-floured tray, brush with the glaze and leave to rise in a warm place for 10–15 minutes.
7. Bake in an oven, preheated to 200°C/Gas 6, for 30–40 minutes. Serve warm or cool with butter.

homemade granola

This delectable recipe for an up-market version of muesli comes from the acclaimed American chef-caterer Ina Garten, known as the Barefoot Contessa. She suggests serving it with yoghurt and berries, or with cold milk.

Makes 24 servings

Ingredients

410g old-fashioned rolled oats

110g sweetened coconut shreds or flakes

240g flaked almonds

150ml vegetable oil (e.g. grapeseed oil)

160g good clear honey

230g small-diced dried apricots

150g small-diced dried figs

110g dried cherries

110g dried cranberries

140g roasted, unsalted cashews

Method

1. Preheat the oven to 180°C/Gas 4.
2. Toss the oats, coconut and almonds together in a large bowl. Whisk together the oil and honey, and pour over the oat mixture. Stir with a wooden spoon until all the oats and nuts are coated.
3. Pour on to a 33cm × 45cm baking sheet (or two smaller ones). Bake, stirring occasionally with a spatula, until the mixture turns a nice, even golden brown (about 45 minutes).
4. Remove the granola from the oven and allow to cool, stirring occasionally.
5. Add the apricots, figs, cherries, cranberries and cashews.
6. Store the cooled granola in an airtight container.

pasta, pastry & flatbreads

1 | 2 | 3 | 4

5 | 6 | 7a | 7b | 8 | 9

10 | 11 | 12

pasta

Good-quality dried pasta is traditionally made using durum (hard wheat) semolina and water – look for the words 'di semola di grano duro' on the label – although richer egg pasta ('all'uovo'), made with eggs rather than water, has grown in popularity. The best pasta is invariably Italian.

Keep a selection of pastas for different uses. Long pasta is best with light, liquid sauces, whereas tubes and many of the fancy shapes now on the market are good at capturing chunky sauces. Being more absorbent, egg pasta goes well with creamy sauces, while oil-based ones are better with normal pasta. Though spinach- or tomato-flavoured pastas may be authentic, most coloured pastas are a gimmick and are shunned by purists, apart from saffron and squid ink pasta which are delicious.

Cook pasta in a large pan of boiling salted water, uncovered, until *al dente*. Drain and dress the pasta immediately, then serve. Avoid non-durum wheat or poor-quality pastas that collapse when cooked. Look for rough surfaces made using traditional bronze dies (*trafila*), indicating authentic, well-made pasta.

1 Lumaconi rigati This ridged, snail-shaped pasta tastes excellent stuffed and baked in tomato sauce, and works well in hearty recipes using meat or game sauces.

2 Macaroni (maccheroni) This curly, tubular pasta (which comes in varying shapes and sizes) is often used baked into pies, such as Greek pastitsio or macaroni cheese, but is also good in chunky vegetable soups, or with a rich aubergine, tomato, garlic and herb sauce.

3 Soup pasta Small pasta shapes add texture and variety to soups, especially vegetable, poultry or meat broths. They cook quickly, so add them 10–15 minutes prior to the end of the soup cooking time.

4 Risi This rice-shaped pasta is often used in soups. Both risi and orzo, which is similar, only slightly larger, can be cooked in stock, as for risotto. Or try cooking either type around a joint of lamb or whole chicken, adding chopped tomatoes, oil and stock; the pasta absorbs the meat juices and becomes tender and crusty by the time the meat is cooked.

5 Orecchiette Literally 'little ears', these small discs are excellent served with leeks, butter, Gorgonzola and parsley, or with fresh sausage meat (ideally Italian), sautéed with cavolo nero, tomatoes, onion and garlic. Or simply with butter, pecorino and black pepper.

6 Penne rigate These ridged tubes are great just with butter, Parmesan and black pepper, but also combine well with sauces such as pizzaiola (garlic, tomatoes, herbs and black olives) and carbonara (pancetta, egg, optional cream and Parmesan). Try them also with butter, garlic, onion, saffron and mascarpone.

7 Tagliatelle Ribbon-like noodles, tagliatelle are often made from egg pasta and sold in nests, and are available in spinach (a) and other flavours, as well as plain (b). A speciality of Bologna, they are traditionally served with a meat-based ragu (Bolognese) sauce. Or use them with rich butter, cheese or egg yolk sauces.

8 Tagliardi These thin pasta rectangles are good with light oil-, cream- or butter-based sauces, or with thin vegetable purées, and have a lovely mouth feel. They even work well mixed with honey, brown sugar and yoghurt, as a dessert.

9 Gnocchi Italian gnocchi, usually sold vac-packed, are small dumplings made of semolina or potatoes and flour. Poached until they float, and then dressed and served straight or baked until sizzling. Potato gnocchi go well with pesto and sizzled pine nuts. Tomato and oregano sauce suits baked semolina gnocchi, as does a wild mushroom, mascarpone and red wine sauce.

10 Tagliolini A flat version of spaghetti (similar to linguine), tagliolini are often used in soups, but can also be used with a light dressing, such as one with olive oil, garlic and herbs. Or use them buttered and

seasoned with rich chicken or red meat stock, and served with that same poultry or meat and herbs.

11 Pappardelle Classically served in Tuscany with game sauces, these broad egg noodles can have either straight or wavy edges. Serve them with chicken liver and sage sauce, tomato and meat ragu-type sauces, or with wild greens, sautéed with garlic, olive oil and grated pecorino.

12 Lasagne The quick-cook sheets of pasta now available need no pre-cooking before they are layered with meat sauce and béchamel for baked lasagne; even so, use a thin sauce for the best results. Try alternating an aubergine and roasted capsicum layer with a béchamel and blue cheese layer, or use seafood in saffron cream sauce layered with buttered spinach.

13 Squid ink spaghetti (pasta nero) Lusciously black, glossy and expensive, this pasta is superb eaten with olive oil, mashed anchovies, garlic and capers; or with squid rings, scallops, garlic, cream and tarragon. Look for pasta with a natural colour additive, which is usually ink from cuttlefish rather than squid, in fact.

14 Chitarra The name refers to the guitar-like instrument used to shape

the pasta. Square in cross-section, this pasta has good 'tooth feel'. It is best served plainly, with butter, garlic and black pepper, or with olive oil, chillies, garlic and parsley.

15 Bucatini Thicker than spaghetti, these long, thin tubes go well with substantial meat, vegetable and cheese sauces; they have a firm texture, so they can also be layered in meat pies and bakes.

16 Capellini This thread-thin pasta, also known as angel's hair pasta and sometimes sold in nests, is simple and quick to cook. Use it with soup-like sauces, or in actual soups. Or even add it to milky desserts, such as sweetened custards.

17 Spaghetti The best-loved pasta around the world, spaghetti excels when served simply, especially with 'aglio e olio' (garlic and extra virgin olive oil) or carbonara. It also goes very well with puttanesca sauce (tomatoes, anchovies, black olives and capers).

18 Fusilli lunghi Twisted like a corkscrew, fusilli lunghi can take a rich aubergine, tomato and herb sauce, or an olive and garlic paste sauce; combinations of anchovy, Parmesan and butter, or cream, garlic and pecorino also work well.

13   14   15   16   17   18

fusilli with arrabbiata sauce
Serves 4

Cook 500g dried fusilli lunghi in boiling salted water
for 12–14 minutes. Meanwhile, pour 4 tablespoons
extra virgin olive oil into a separate pan and add
4 chopped shallots, 2 chopped garlic cloves and 75g
preserved red peppers (chopped). Stir in 40 black
olives, 2 tablespoons dried arrabbiata mix (see page
68), 8 tablespoons tomato passata, 6 tablespoons
water and 8 chopped gherkins. When the pasta is
tender, drain and then toss it in the sauce and serve
with Parmesan.

penne with olive, mint and pine nut sauce
Serves 4

Cook 500g penne until *al dente* (9–12 minutes).
Drain, reserving 4 tablespoons of the cooking water.
Meanwhile, fry together 1 chopped onion and 2
chopped garlic cloves in 2 tablespoons extra virgin
olive oil. Push these to one side of the pan. Add 50g
pine nuts, and cook until lightly golden; remove the
nuts and reserve. Stir in 150g black olive paste or
tapenade, 4 tablespoons pasta water, a handful of
torn fresh mint, and salt and freshly ground black
pepper. Toss the drained, cooked pasta into the sauce,
and stir. Serve hot, adding the pine nuts, a squeeze of
lemon juice and extra mint, if liked.

gnocchi in caper pesto
Serves 3–4

Put 2 handfuls flat-leaf parsley, 1 handful mint or
tarragon and 6 chopped spring onions in a food
processor and whiz until blended. Add 40 salted
capers (rinsed and dried), 4–6 crushed garlic cloves,
6 salted anchovies in oil (chopped), 2 tablespoons
Dijon mustard, 2 tablespoons white wine vinegar and
2 tablespoons lemon juice; whiz again. Cook 500g
potato gnocchi in boiling water, drain, and combine
them with enough sauce to coat. Bake in an oven,
preheated to 220°C/ Gas 8, for 15–25 minutes, then
serve alone, or with a fresh tomato salad. Any extra,
unused sauce can be refrigerated for up to 4 days.

pappardelle with luganega sausage sauce
Serves 4

Remove the casings from 350g luganega sausages
(or other coarse Italian sausage). Chop and stir-fry
the meat in 1 tablespoon lard or butter, adding
1 chopped onion, 3 chopped garlic cloves and
4 chopped fresh sage leaves. Add 100ml white wine,
then mash in 25g mascarpone and 1 teaspoon dried
oregano. Stir, and simmer for 8 minutes. Meanwhile,
cook 500g pappardelle for 6–8 minutes, drain, and
mix with the sauce. Finally, heat 4 tablespoons extra
virgin olive oil, and add 8 chopped sage leaves; when
sizzling, pour a little of the oil over each serving.

squid ink pasta with seafood sauce

This superb seafood sauce, which flatters the black squid ink spaghetti or tagliatelle outrageously well, is based on the classic Italian dish, *frutti di mare in bianco*. It is a wonderfully quick recipe: the fish is minimally cooked, and the sauce reduces while the pasta is cooking.

Serves 4

Ingredients

200g (or 8) whole baby squid, washed and drained
200g salmon fillet, in 25g pieces
250g monkfish, in 30g pieces
1kg fresh, live mussels, scrubbed
150ml Sauvignon Blanc
1 onion, chopped
4 garlic cloves
75g salted butter
250g dried squid ink spaghetti or tagliatelle
4 tbsp single cream
1 tbsp potato flour
fresh parsley, to garnish

Method

1. Prepare the squid by cutting off the tentacle section in front of the eyes, and set aside. Squeeze out any squid ink, then pull out and discard the eye area and the body contents. Remove and discard the backbone.
2. Slice the body into 2cm slices. Set aside with the tentacles. Pat dry the salmon and monkfish pieces.
3. Put the mussels in a heavy pan, along with the wine, onion, garlic and half of the butter. Cover the pan and cook over medium-high heat for 4–5 minutes, or until the mussels begin to open. Remove the mussels as they open, continuing to cook the remaining ones, covered, until all are opened. Discard any mussels that remain closed. Reserve the liquid.
4. Cook the pasta in lots of boiling salted water, uncovered, for 12–15 minutes, until *al dente*.
5. Meanwhile, put the squid, salmon and monkfish in the pan with the remaining butter. Cook gently for 3–4 minutes, or until the fish is firm and opaque. Remove using a slotted spoon. Keep hot, along with the cooked mussels.
6. Boil the wine-fish liquid until reduced and flavourful. Add the cream and the butter from cooking the fish.
7. Mix the potato flour with 2 tablespoons cold water. Pour this into the fish sauce. Shake and swirl the pan over high heat until thickened. Replace the cooked seafood in the pan and reheat until all is hot again.
8. Serve the pasta hot with equal shares of the fish, sauce and parsley, ideally with some chilled Sauvignon Blanc.

noodles

What most distinguishes Asian noodles from European pasta is the diversity of the starches from which they are made. Some are sold, ready-to-eat, in vac-packs, but dried noodles have a long shelf life and take only minutes to prepare: many need only brief cooking or short immersion in hand-hot or near-boiling water. Cooking instructions on the packet can be useful, but use your own judgement: texture and mouth feel are the chief charms of good noodles.

1 Udon These thick Japanese wheat noodles should be cooked in boiling water for 1–2 minutes (or 10–12 minutes for dried noodles) until soft but chewy, and then rinsed. Often eaten in bowls of dashi or miso broth, udon noodles can also be eaten in less traditional fashion, with chicken, hoisin, light soy sauce and herbs, for example.

2 Soba These buckwheat and wheat flour noodles from Japan are delicate, nutty and delicious. Cook them for five minutes until tender and rinse. Serve them with miso or dashi stock, hot or spicy accompaniments and Asian condiments.

3 Somen Thin Japanese wheat noodles, somen should have a firm, chewy texture and are normally served chilled. After cooking in boiling water (two to three minutes), rinse, cool and serve them with chilled broth, or try them with shredded nori, wasabi and radishes.

4 Mung bean noodles Made from mung bean flour, and sometimes called cellophane or glass noodles, these are fine but tough. Put them into a bowl, cover with near-boiling water, and watch them turn opaque in a few minutes. Serve them with hot broth and other accompaniments, or in a stir-fry. They are also good in wraps and spring rolls.

5 Thai rice noodles Sold in handy bundles, these hair-thin rice noodles need to be rehydrated in hand-hot water or briefly cooked in hot stock until softened and opaque. They can also be deep-fried. Add them to laksa soups or clear broths, or stir-fry them with prawns, sweet-sour sauces or fish sauce, mint, chilli, ginger and garlic.

6 Rice vermicelli Fine Chinese rice vermicelli should be soaked – in hand-hot water for five minutes or in cold water for 20 minutes – until pliable and opaque. Use them in cooked dishes, dressed in hot, spicy sauces and with textural additions, such as leafy vegetables, salted peanuts, Sichuan peppercorns or fresh ginger.

7 Rice stick noodles Made from rice flour, these Thai or Vietnamese noodles can be rehydrated in boiling water for one or two minutes (too long and they'll flop). Medium rice sticks (a) are about 5mm wide, and thick rice sticks (b) about 1cm. They can be served with sauces or in broths (try them in Thai green curry broth with prawns, crunchy vegetables and greens), or reheated in stir-fries.

8 Chinese wheat noodles These yellowish noodles need brief rehydration or cooking in hot liquids for three to ten minutes (the time can vary hugely). Try them with black or yellow bean sauce, tofu, bean sprouts and crunchy toppings.

9 Dried egg noodles These Chinese noodles, made from wheat flour and egg, come in many thicknesses and are often folded into sheets. Cook them by adding to light broths for about five minutes; serve in a broth, with additions such as lap cheung (see page 79); they can also be used in pad thai.

sichuan prawn chow mein

This noodle recipe, by the renowned Southeast Asian food authority, Sri Owen, maximises flavours, colours and textures, and is also extremely easy to make. "I have been asked many times why I have never put a chow mein recipe in any of my books. Chow mein simply means 'fried noodles', so evidently the time has come to produce this recipe, which otherwise I would simply have called 'Sichuan prawn fried noodles'."

Serves 4

Ingredients
24 large king prawns, uncooked, shelled, cut in half lengthwise and deveined
salt
125ml groundnut oil, for frying
4 shallots, finely chopped
2 tsp finely chopped ginger root
1 tsp sugar
2 garlic cloves, very thinly sliced
4 spring onions, cut into thin rounds
1 tsp Sichuan peppercorns, finely crushed, or 1 tsp chilli powder
1 tbsp Chinese rice wine or dry sherry
1 tbsp soy sauce
3 tomatoes, skinned and chopped
½ tsp freshly ground black pepper
225–350g egg noodles, cooked, refreshed under cold water and drained
2 tbsp chopped fresh coriander

Method
1. Rub the halved prawns with ½ teaspoon salt and keep them in the fridge while you prepare the spice mixture.
2. Heat 2 tablespoons of the oil in a wok. Fry the shallots and ginger for 2 minutes. Add the sugar and garlic, and stir-fry for 1 minute more. Then add the remaining ingredients – except the prawns, the remaining oil, the noodles and coriander – together with salt to taste. Continue stir-frying for 2 more minutes.
3. Heat the remaining oil in a frying pan and, when hot, fry the prawns, stirring them all the time, for about 2 minutes. Remove them with a wire scoop and transfer to a tray lined with kitchen paper.
4. Put the noodles into a conical sieve and pour boiling water over them for 5–10 seconds, and drain well. Stir them into the contents of the wok and mix well. Add the prawns and coriander leaves, and go on stir-frying for 1 minute longer. Serve immediately.

pastry and wrappers

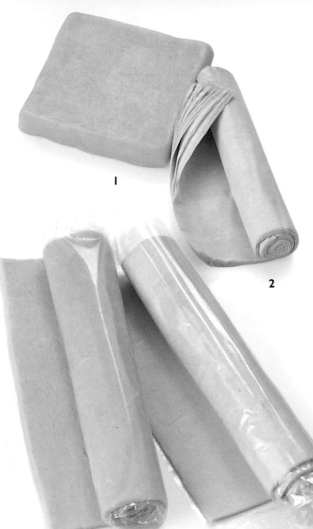

The world of pastry is one of high artistry, but it is open to anyone if they buy ready-made pastry and wrappers. Both European and Asian pastries are essentially vehicles, enclosing, wrapping or providing layers for other foods. European pastry is often baked in the oven (ideally, in a fan oven and on a heavy, dark, metal tray, which conducts heat well) or deep-fried. Thin, fine Asian wrappers, on the other hand, can be poached, steamed, fried or braised, or a combination of these methods.

Although many fresh pastries and wrappers are perishable once opened, many are now so effectively packaged that they last in any cool, dark place for at least several days, and sometimes much longer. Pastries also freeze well: thaw them briefly before they are needed (unused wrappers can be refrozen safely).

1 Pâte sucrée This is basically shortcrust pastry that has been enriched with egg yolks, extra butter and sugar. It is sold for use in French-style desserts, tartlets and small sweet (and even some savoury) pastries. Roll it out, chilled, on a floured surface, and try it in tarte aux poires or individual banoffee tarts.

2 Filo pastry This Greek, flour-and-water pastry is stretched until it is so thin that you can read print through it. It is sold in rectangular sheets, usually rolled, and can be kept pliable while in use by being covered with thick plastic wrap and a damp cloth. Brushed with melted butter or olive oil, and in many layers wrapped around fillings, it cooks to crunchy golden crispness.

Filo suits Greek, Turkish and Middle Eastern sweet and savoury fillings. Use it for Greek tiropittas (cheese triangles) or galacto-boureko (vanilla cream pie), for example. It can also be substituted for other similar pastries, such as *brique*, *yufka*, *ouarka* and *malsouka*.

3 Puff pastry Most of the fat in this pastry is not in the dough mixture itself but is spread on to the rolled-out pastry before it is folded into its many and characteristic layers to be baked at a high temperature: the result is a light and crisp pastry, puffed up to many times its original volume. While it is possible to make puff pastry at home, it is much easier to buy the bought version, either ready rolled (a) or as a block (b), which tastes good and is superbly quick.

Use puff pastry with sweet or savoury fillings: for Middle Eastern triangular meat, nut or spice pastries, for example, or pithiviers (a French tart filled with a sweet almondy filling).

4 Shortcrust pastry Though easy to make at home, buying ready-made rolls (a) or blocks (b) of shortcrust pastry can save time and effort. This simple pastry is made from flour, fats (butter and/or lard), and water; if chilled, it is easy to shape. Use it for single- or double-crust pies and tarts, which are often brushed with egg before cooking. For quiches, the pastry case is best baked blind first, and then rebaked with the filling. Shortcrust pastry can also be used for Latin American empanadas, for frying or baking.

5

7

8

6

9

5 Rice paper wrappers Called *bahn trang* in Vietnamese, these wrappers come in quarter-circles or discs, They must be softened before being filled: brush both sides with warm water or dip them briefly in water. Add one to two tablespoons of crunchy Vietnamese-style stuffing, roll the wrapper up tight, and then eat with no further cooking. Serve with a Vietnamese-style salad and good dipping sauces, such as *nuoc mam*, sweet chilli or soy sauce.

6 Kataifi pastry This intriguing wheat pastry is most commonly used in Greek or Turkish sticky pastries. The flexible shreds can be rolled or wrapped around a food, or made into nests and filled with dried fruit or nuts, before being drizzled with melted butter or ghee and then baked; syrups are often poured over before serving. Or fill the pastry with chicken, fish, lamb or prawns, bake and drizzle with a sweet-sour dressing.

7 Peking duck wrappers These fine rice-flour wrappers, or pancakes, should be brushed with sesame oil and layered in a steamer or foil-lined colander, to be warmed before being served with lacquered duck shreds and green herbs, hoisin and chilli sauces and salad. Or substitute crab or ham shreds. Have Asian sauces nearby for dipping.

8 Wonton wrappers Silky wonton wrappers or 'skins' (made of wheat flour) are usually square, but can be trimmed easily, with scissors, to round. Filled and folded into various shapes, as dumplings, they suit deep-frying, though they can also be steamed or boiled in a broth. Wonton skins can also be used to make spring rolls. Or use two wrappers with a filling for a non-traditional ravioli-style dish.

9 Strudel pastry This paper-thin, stretchy, wheat-flour pastry, a more supple version of filo pastry, is sold in sheets or rolls. It should be brushed with butter, filled and then baked. Good strudel fillings include apples, spices and crumbs, cherries with cinnamon, and sweet seed and nut fillings. Superb strudels are made in Germany, Austria, Hungary and other Central European countries.

10 Chinese dumpling wrappers These creamy-white wrappers (also called Gyozo wrappers) are thicker than wonton skins, and are best braised or steamed. Fill them with a sesame chicken stuffing; with minced pork, ginger, garlic, cream, black beans and parsley; or with dried and fresh prawns minced with coriander, spring onions, carrot and aromatics. Serve the dumplings as snacks with dipping sauces and tea.

10

kataifi fruit-nut pastries
Serves 4–8

Twist 8 handfuls kataifi pastry into 8 neat nests. Set on an oiled baking sheet and bake for 40 minutes at 200°C/Gas 6, or until crisp. Mix 4 tablespoons scented stock syrup (see page 44) or clear honey with 8 tablespoons melted ghee or butter. Spoon some over each nest. Combine 6 prunes, 25g each dried apricots, cherries, cranberries and mixed nuts, and 75g diced marzipan with 4 tablespoons pomegranate molasses together in a food processor. Pulse until roughly chopped. Pile some on each kataifi nest. Increase the heat to 220°C/Gas 7 and bake until golden: 15–20 minutes. Serve drizzled with a syrup of honey, lemon juice and cinnamon stick pieces.

chorizo puff pastry bracelets
Makes about 20

Roll out 400g puff pastry to 3mm thickness. Spread one side of the pastry with 3 tablespoons harissa paste mixed with 3 tablespoons tomato paste. Scissor-chop 50g sliced chorizo and sprinkle it over the paste. Fold the uncovered half of the pastry over the covered surface. Press it closed and roll again. Slice the filled pastry into 1cm strips and tie each strip loosely, twisting the long ends around the loop to form 'bracelets'. Bake these at 200°C/Gas 6 for 18–20 minutes, or until crisp. Serve hot, with chilled fino or amontillado sherry.

bahn trang wraps with peanuts and spicy dip

Serves 4

Assemble 8 large rice paper wrappers (*bahn trang*) and a selection of fillings, such as boiled lap cheung sausages, bamboo shoots, straw mushrooms, spring onions, parsley or coriander, yellow miso and carrot shreds. Soften each wrapper in warm water for 30–40 seconds, then drain. Enclose a portion of filling in each wrapper. Wrap each in cling film and chill until required. Slice diagonally in half, unwrap, and serve on mung bean noodles with a choice of moist and dry dipping accompaniments.

steamed and fried wontons

Makes 24

Have ready 32 square wonton wrappers. Then, make a filling by food-processing together, briefly: 100g minced pork, lamb or chicken, 2 teaspoons dark sesame oil, 5cm fresh ginger (grated), 2 mashed garlic cloves, 4 spinach leaves, 50g tofu and 2 tablespoons bacon fat or double cream. Divide this filling into 32 balls. Centre 16 of these on 16 of the wrappers. Fold two points together, making a triangle, and wet the two narrowest corners. With the base of the triangle towards you, bring each of the corners across two-thirds of the base line, like a mitre, to seal. Steam for 4–6 minutes, until firm. With the rest of the filling, set 2 filling portions in the centre of each of 8 dampened wrappers and press another wrapper neatly on top. Deep-fry these envelopes until crisp. Serve with a dipping sauce.

flatbreads

The first flatbreads were probably made by spreading flour batters or doughs over fire-heated stones until they dried and crisped. Some are still made this way today. Many of these breads are useful in all sorts of ways, not only as snacks in their own right. They can be steam-dampened or wetted and used as wrappers; they can be pulled apart into pieces and stuffed or layered to create more complex dishes; or slit and filled with savoury or sweet fillings. If sautéed or shallow fried in oil, lard, butter or ghee, many become luxurious. Others are good oven-crisped, to be used, hot, as a vehicle for softer foods.

1 Lavash This pliable, nutty-sweet Middle Eastern bread is sold in large, thin sheets that are usually folded into squares. Dampened and reheated briefly, lavash can be eaten with hummus or babaganoush; with dukkah and olive oil; with kukuye (omelette) or spicy lamb kebabs. Filled with cheese and retoasted, it makes a good sandwich.

2 Buckwheat galettes (galettes de sarrasin) Originally from Brittany, these brownish pancakes are traditionally made of sourish and nutty buckwheat flour. Dampen and reheat them briefly in a frying pan, add ham and an egg, and then refold: delicious. Or try them, more unusually, with butter, cooked apples and Calvados.

3 Tortillas Much imitated around the world, these Mexican flatbreads are authentically made from masa harina (see page 136), although wheat-flour tortillas also exist. Good tortillas are soft, supple and fragrant once briefly warmed, and can be used to mop up mashed refried beans, guacamole, or spicy chicken, beef or pork; or can be stuffed and rolled as enchiladas.

4 Chapati (roti) These unleavened breads, eaten all over India and Pakistan, are made from whole-wheat flour, and should be tender and speckled. Reheat them briefly, and tear off pieces to dip into soups or to scoop up curries and other hot Indian dishes.

5 Naan (nan) Many types of naan bread are made throughout Asia, but in the West it refers to the North Indian leavened bread served in any Indian restaurant. This is a puffy, soft bread, usually made of wheat flour, leavening, milk or yoghurt and seasonings. Traditionally cooked in a clay tandoor (oven), naan bread has a characteristic smoky taste. Eat it with dhals, curries, coconut rice and spicy chickpea dishes.

6 Poppadoms These crisp Indian wafers can be bought as

uncooked sheets (pictured). Cook them in hot oil, or grill or even microwave them, until puffed up and crisp. In the West, they are eaten with chutneys and relishes as an appetiser; in India they are eaten at the end of a meal.

7 Pitta bread Flattish and round or oval, pittas are the most widely available breads in the eastern Mediterranean, and are integral to central and west Asian meals. Available as either plain (white) or wholewheat, warm pitta can be slit open to create pockets and are perfect for foods such as felafel and salad with tahini sauce or Greek pork souvlaki.

8 Waffles (gaufres) Honeycomb-textured batter cakes, cooked in waffle irons, usually come from Holland, Belgium, France or the United States. Bought waffles are best toasted or quick-baked and eaten with jam, ice cream, maple syrup, or simply butter. In the United States, they are served with bacon, eggs and maple syrup.

9 Pumpernickel (Schwartzbrot) This famous, wholegrain rye bread from Westphalia in Germany is leavened by a sourdough culture; its dark colour is a result of the caramelisation of the rye during baking. Often sold sliced in rectangular blocks, it is superb as the base for open sandwiches. Eat it with cheese, smoked sausage, or Black Forest ham and berry preserves.

10 Pikelets These traditional British yeast-leavened pancakes, griddle-cooked and with holes patterning the upper surface, are delicious eaten warm with berry jam and clotted cream, or with cream cheese and currant jelly. Drop scones and Scottish pancakes are similar.

11 Irish potato farls Mashed potato and flour combined in the proportion of 4:1 make a delicious damp bread, traditionally cooked as cakes, or triangular farls, on a griddle. Serve the cakes toasted and buttered with soft or hard cheeses, smoked fish in cream or sausages.

12 Blini These small Russian buckwheat, yeast-raised pancakes are traditionally served warm with caviar or cured fish, often with soured cream or melted butter. They are also excellent with taramosalata.

13 Carta da mùsica These large Sardinian flatbreads, made of hard wheat flour, are delicious either brushed with olive oil and then baked or grilled until hot and crunchy, or plain, with olive, aubergine or chickpea pastes. Alternatively, soften pieces in water, to be used like softened pasta for layering in baked dishes or to wrap around a spicy filling.

savoury biscuits

Crackers, wafers and other savoury biscuits are usually crisp or crumbly ('short') in texture, flour-based, and either baked or fried. While designed for use as snacks, these biscuits can be broken, crushed or powdered for other uses, whether as a crispy topping, or as a crumb-crust base for savoury cheesecakes or tartlets, or to give crunch to soft salads. They are superbly useful.

1 Bruschettini Dried, oven-crisped slices of bruschetta can be crushed finely as a gratin topping for sliced aubergines or lasagne, or coarsely crushed for use in meatballs. They can also be dampened with olive oil and used as the basis of Italy's famous panzanella salad.

2 Matzo crackers Made of flour and water, this unleavened Jewish bread is crisp and flaky. The crackers can be crushed and used as bread-crumbs for toppings and coverings.

3 Scandinavian rye crispbreads These biscuits are thick, strong and crusty but light, low in fat and high in fibre. Eat them with cured meats and hard cheeses, or break them up into hot milk and add honey, for a quick, unorthodox breakfast.

4 Scottish oatcakes Shaped into rounds or triangles (farls), these biscuits are so brittle that Scots usually lay (rather than spread) butter on top of them. They can be crumbled over baked vegetables or into barley and vegetable soups.

5 High-baked water biscuits Dark-dappled water biscuits have a distinctive, toasty taste and a hard yet flaky texture. Crushed to fragments or a powder, they can be used, with savoury spices, as part of a mixture to scatter on potato-topped cottage pies before baking.

6 Scottish rye wafers These scrumptious hexagonal wafers, sometimes dotted with seeds, are good with both sweet and savoury spreads. Try sandwiching them together in pairs with cream cheese and smoked salmon.

7 Saltines Perforated for easy breaking, these biscuits are found worldwide. Baked hard and dry, they were once a staple food for sailors on long voyages, and are still known as ship's biscuits. Use them to accompany fish or corn chowder.

8 Rice cakes These spongy, low-fat and gluten-free biscuits can be utterly flavourless or delicious. The best are flavoured with sesame, soy sauce, salt or seaweed. Try crumbling them, to mix with dried fruit and nuts, like muesli, or to add extra texture to salads.

9 Prawn crackers Flavoured with prawn or fish, these deep-fried crackers are delicious if made in Indonesia; Chinese versions are more variable in quality. Eat them with fresh, spicy relishes or sambals, or with coconut-based fish dishes.

10 Melba toasts These wheat-flour toasts do not break or soften quickly if buttered. They can be crushed and used, with cayenne and melted butter, as a crumb base for savoury cheesecakes, or as a tasty coating for fish cakes.

11 Cheese wafer thins Very cheesy, these flaky Dutch biscuits are much copied but rarely bettered. Roughly crushed, they make a gratin topping. Finely crushed, they add colour, texture and savour to smoked fish pies or cauliflower cheese. Or toast them briefly and crumble them over a soft cheese and watercress salad.

flours &
cooking aids

flours and thickening agents

Flours can be used to make everything from bread to puddings, to thicken sauces, to add crispness to fried foods: they are multifunctional. Although flour can be made from all sorts of starchy foods, on its own the word usually means wheat flour. Wheat (*Triticum*) is special in that it contains gluten (a stretchy protein that helps make dough light and airy). Flour exists in thousands of varieties – many common wheat flours are varieties of *Triticum aestivum* – all containing different amounts of gluten: high-gluten hard wheat flours are used to make bread, while low-gluten soft wheat flours are used for cakes; so it is usually important to match the right flour to the recipe.

Starchy thickening agents must usually be mixed (or slaked) in a little cold water before being added to a hot liquid, to avoid the formation of lumps, or else mixed to a paste with butter.

I White flour Highly milled white, or plain, flour from soft or medium wheat grain is good for most purposes. The fine grains can absorb large quantities of liquid and sugar, which produces a softer finish perfect for cakes, doughs, sauces and batters. 'Cake' flour, common in the United States, is a specially treated plain flour that is super-soft and very absorbent. Self-raising flour, popular in Britain, is plain white flour with raising agents added.

Italian doppio zero flour (00, or 'double-zero', flour) is a soft white flour perfect for making pasta at home (most soft wheat flours make only passable pasta dough), particularly in combination with semolina.

2 Strong white flour (bread flour) This flour suits bread-making because it is made from a hard variety of *Triticum aestivum* that is high in gluten; additional gluten may also be added. The elasticity of the gluten is activated by kneading, and gives bread its characteristic, fibrous structure once it is baked.

3 Buckwheat flour Ground buckwheat is used in Russian blini, Breton crêpes, and in breakfast pancakes in parts of the United States. It has a fairly strong, nutty and astringent taste, which is not to everyone's liking. Combining it half and half with wheat flour is a good option.

4 Polenta flour This finely ground maize flour is a finer version of cornmeal or polenta (see page 107). It adds sweetness, colour and protein to cornbreads, country breads, pancakes, dessert cakes and biscuits; it is used in Portugal's famous yeast-raised cornbreads.

5 Masa harina This unusual, lime-treated, precooked flour, made from ground corn, is essential in Mexican cuisine and has a distinctive taste and putty-like texture when mixed to a dough. Rolled or pressed flat, masa harina dough makes tortillas. The flour can also be used for tamale dough, steamed, or to bind mixtures or coat foods for frying.

6 Coarse-grain flour (granary)
Though the name 'granary' is a proprietary term, it is commonly used to describe nutty, toasty, three-wheat flour with malted grains. Use it for breads, scones, batters, malt bread and even cakes.

7 Ground rice This sandy-textured flour, made from polished white rice, is used in many Jewish, Indian, Middle Eastern and European dishes. As well as thickening milky puddings, soups and stews, ground rice helps produce crispness in batters, doughs, cakes and biscuits. Try it in *keskül* (Turkish almond custard) and Scottish shortbread.

8 Gram flour Made of ground chickpeas or other dried peas or beans, this nutty flour is popular in India, and parts of Italy and France. Chickpea flour is used, famously, in socca (pancakes sold in the streets of Provence). In India, gram flour is used in fritters and savoury breads. It contains next to no gluten.

9 Spelt flour This ancient form of wheat, which still thrives in the Balkans, has complex, lively flavours, and is less genetically modified than ordinary wheat flours. When used in bread dough, spelt flour rises quicker than usual, but collapses if left to rise for too long.

10 Wholemeal flour This flour is made from the whole wheat grain, including both the bran (fibrous outer layer) and the nutritious germ. ('Brown' or wheatmeal flour has some bran and germ extracted.) Wholemeal flour may be made of soft or hard wheat, the latter being used to make strong wholemeal flour for bread-making. Stoneground flours, using traditional millstones rather than rollers, are the best: the flour is coarser but has a better flavour and mouth feel.

11 Chestnut flour (farina di castagne) Once important in certain rural areas of France and Italy, this sweet chestnut flour is gluten-free, starchy and protein-rich, so it adds density and richness to batters, doughs and cakes. Try it in bitter chocolate puddings or in flattish country breads, mixed with spelt flour or strong bread flour.

thickening agents

12 Cornflour (cornstarch) This is often used to thicken sauces, gravies, casseroles and milky desserts. Its main problem is that it can turn gelatinous and look cloudy rather than remaining clear and smooth. However, it does not break down when frozen, so is useful for stews to be frozen. Cornflour, when used 1:3 with wheat flour, can also lighten cakes, batters and some biscuits.

13 Arrowroot This super-fine powder, from the Maranta plant, produces a soft, stable, crystal-clear gel, which makes great glazes for peach or apricot tarts, clear sauces for poached chicken breast, or shiny sauces for spareribs of pork. Once slaked in cold water and stirred into hot liquid, arrowroot cooks quickly: remove the liquid from the heat straight away, or it may thin again.

14 Tapioca starch This fine starch made from cassava (manioc) root is often used in Asian dishes, to thicken meat mixtures, coconut or dairy milk sauces, soups and desserts, or to help create smooth batters for pancakes and omelettes. Mixed with water, it can also thicken stock or fruit-based sauces.

15 Tapioca These curious, hard grains are starch granules extracted from cassava root. Cooked in dilute liquids, they soften, swell and gelatinise, thereby thickening the cooking liquid, so that it sets. Many Scandinavian and Asian desserts, fruit soups and drinks contain tapioca. Tapioca 'pearls' (pictured) are larger than normal tapioca, and require soaking for two to three hours in cold water before use.

16 Rice starch Made from glutinous rice and much finer than ground rice, this thickener makes an elegant and crispy surface coating for foods to be steamed or fried. Use it to lighten doughs, cakes and batters (it keeps deep-fried squid crunchy), and to thicken delicate dessert sauces.

17 Custard powder This yellow powder contains cornflour, salt, flavouring and annatto. As well as being used for custard (ideally with added sugar, egg yolks and cream), it is also good for creating a stable, glossy gel for butterscotch, caramel or mocha sauces.

18 Potato flour Also called fécule or fecula, this delicate potato starch is a useful thickener. It needs only 40–50 seconds' cooking time, and gives a sheer, glossy effect. It can be used, with egg and milk, to make tiny potato pancakes, and can improve the texture of potato bread and dumplings. Use it 1:2 with wheat flour for lighter cakes.

19 Purple yam flour This pretty flour, made from dried and ground yams, works well in sticky, thickened desserts, as well as in some Philipino doughs and cakes.

20 Kuzu (kudzu) A dense Japanese thickener, made from the roots of a vine, kuzu tends to clump in its raw state into odd angular shapes, but these can be crushed using a pestle and mortar. It is excellent for giving gloss and body to vegetable stews, or for dry-coating thin pork, fish or chicken strips before deep-frying, to produce a light and crispy surface.

storage

Store flour airtight, on a cool, dark, dry and airy shelf. Plain flour can keep for up to six months, but wholemeal flour is best used within two months, since the oil in the germ tends to go rancid. Buy small volumes, often.

cooking aids

While some of these intriguing items have only occasional relevance, many can greatly improve the taste, consistency, looks or authenticity of a dish. Some, such as cochineal, are merely cosmetic; others, such as baking powder or gelatine, are structural components that utterly identify a particular recipe or improve the ease of making it.

The effectiveness of some cooking aids, particularly raising agents, wanes over time. Always check the 'best before' date, and store in a cool, dark and dry place.

1 Glycerine This sticky syrup is useful to help retain moistness, gloss and softness in foods such as glacéed and crystallised fruits. It is also valuable for delaying the setting of cake icings when undertaking time-consuming decoration. Only tiny amounts are needed.

2 Vegetable rennet This liquid coagulant is a vegetarian version of the more traditional rennet enzyme found in the stomachs of ruminants. It is used to set milk-based mixtures into curds and whey for the dessert called junket: about 10 drops will set 550ml of tepid milk (at 32°C). Try it for almond or vanilla and rose water junket.

3 Glucose syrup A synonym for dextrose, glucose syrup can be used to modify crystallisation in

home-made 'soft-scoop' ice creams, to create nougatine (a pliable form of nougat), or as edible 'glue', for attaching cake decorations.

4 Cochineal An intense red liquid food colouring produced by crushing an insect found on Central American cacti can be useful for creating pink icing for cakes or red cherry pie glaze. (The nearest vegetable red pigment equivalents include beetroot juice or, better still, red sorrel.)

5 Baking powder Cream of tartar and bicarbonate of soda used to be the standard raising agents, but now ready-made baking powders are more common. This type requires heat as well as liquid to be activated, so any delay between mixing and baking is not disastrous.

6 Bicarbonate of soda Also known as sodium bicarbonate or baking soda, this alkaline powder, mixed with acid (such as cream of tartar or lemon juice), produces carbon dioxide to 'raise' flour mixtures; it should be mixed in just before baking since otherwise the gas dissipates. Adding bicarbonate of soda to the water when cooking dried pulses can soften the skins and make them easier to digest.

7 Cream of tartar This mildly acidic powder, used 2:1 with an alkali such as bicarbonate of soda, creates a homemade baking powder that activates on mixing with liquid. A pinch can improve the volume and lightness when whisking egg whites for meringues, and discourage the formation of crystals in sugar syrups during cooking.

8 Ascorbic acid (vitamin C) This crystalline powder, available from chemists, can speed up rising when using yeast in bread doughs. It also helps to preserve naturally vivid colours, such as the red pigments in strawberry jam, as well as to safeguard vitamin levels and boost flavours. Add some to home-made lemonade, or to blackcurrant or raspberry coulis or sauces.

9 Fast-acting yeast Also known as micronised yeast, this powder-fine yeast, sold in 7g sachets, is the equivalent of 15g of fresh yeast, or one tablespoon of regular dry yeast. The huge advantage of fast-acting yeast is that, unlike fresh yeast or granules, it is added directly to the flour and no waiting is needed.

10 Gelatine Made from animal hides and bones, this setting agent can be used to set fruit or wine jellies, aspics and mousses. Both granulated gelatine (a) and leaf or sheet gelatine (b) need to be softened in cold liquid before being heated over boiling water until clear (they must not boil), and then whisked into the (ideally warmed) liquid to be set. Let cool and then chill for two to six hours, to set.

11 Rice paper This papery, edible base for sweets and confections is made of the pithy stems of a Chinese shrub. Use it as a surface on which to mould, pipe or place sticky, fragile or delicate chocolate, toffee, caramel, marshmallow or fudge mixtures, or for macaroons.

12 Agar-agar This setting agent, made from seaweed, is popular in Asian cooking and useful for vegetarians who would rather not use animal-based gelatine. Available either as granules (a) or strands (b), agar-agar can be simply stirred into the liquid to be set, boiled briefly (agar-agar will dissolve only in boiling water), and then stirred until thickened. Cool and leave to set. Less agar-agar than gelatine is needed to set the same volume of liquid.

13 Panko (Japanese breadcrumbs) The best bought breadcrumbs are these light Japanese crumbs, sold either coarse (pictured) or fine. They are used to coat sliced and egg-dipped seafood, fish or meat for frying (for Japanese furai dishes), but are so light that they can be used in cake recipes. They can also make 'instant' bread sauce with milk and ground cloves. Sautéed in butter they are delicious on noodles, too.

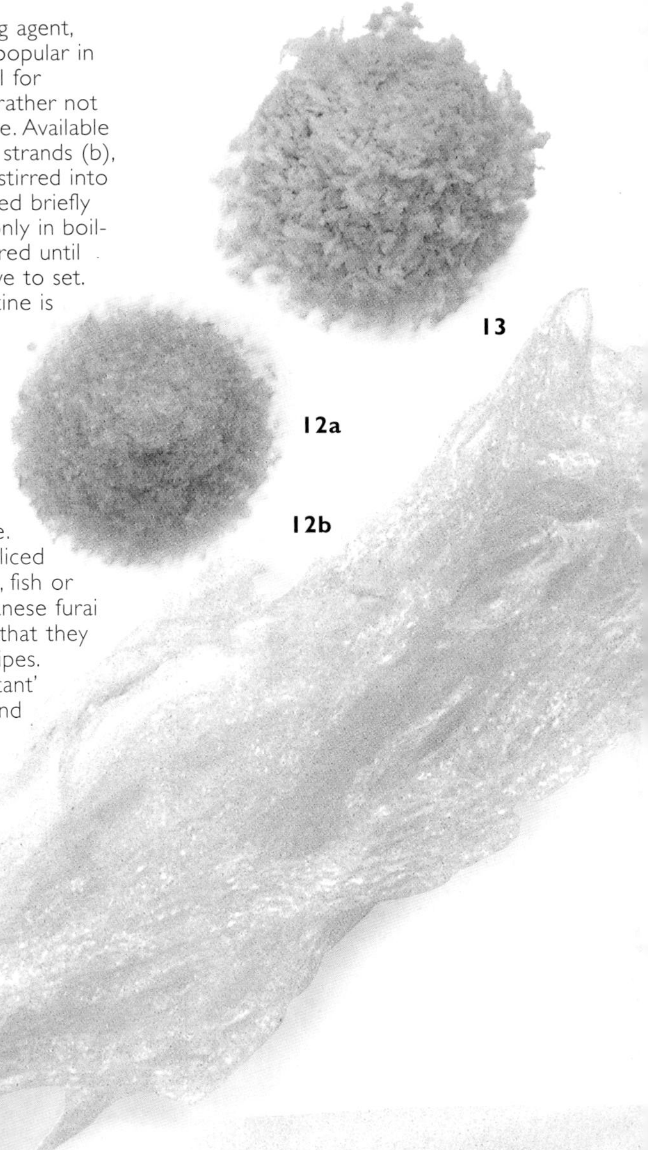

13

12a

12b

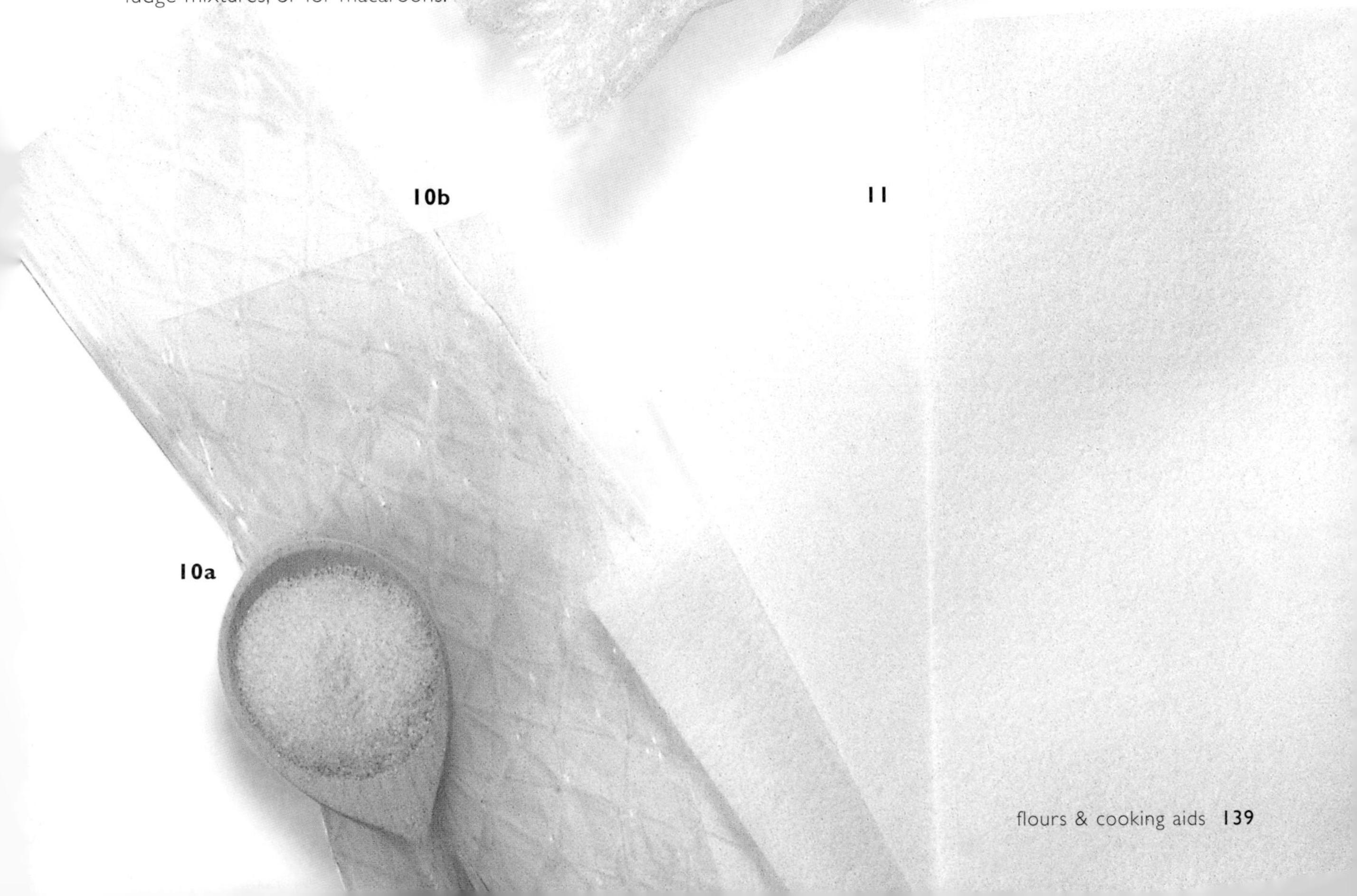

10b

11

10a

sweet scones

Makes 6–8

Baking powder, as well as self-raising flour, is the secret of good scones, as is quick, minimal handling. Mix together 300g self-raising flour, 2 teaspoons baking powder, a pinch of salt and 25g caster sugar. Rub in 75g butter, cubed, until the mixture looks like coarse breadcrumbs. Whisk together 1 egg and 100ml milk. Stir into the dry ingredients to form a soft dough. Turn the dough out and knead it lightly, using floured fingertips (not a rolling pin), to about 2.5 cm thickness. Cut into 6–8 rounds. Bake in an oven, preheated to 230°C/Gas 8, for 10–12 minutes, or until crusty and golden. Cool slightly on a rack. Serve warm with butter, strawberry jam and crème fraîche or other thick cream.

cranberry tapioca and cream

Serves 4

This old-fashioned recipe is updated by the use of a microwave oven; it uses cranberry juice drink, which has a long shelf life and a great colour. Mix 75g tapioca (if you use the large pearls, these must be soaked in water for 3 to 8 hours first), rinsed, and 300ml cranberry juice drink in a large heatproof jug. Stir well, cover with a plate and microwave on High for 20 minutes, stirring after 10 minutes. Stir in 4–6 tablespoons of granulated sugar and another 150ml cranberry juice. Cook for a further 10 minutes, or until no hard white centres are visible in the tapioca, and it feels soft and jelly-like. Stir in 120ml extra cranberry drink, and also 1 tablespoon dark rum, brandy or Cointreau. Pour into 4 serving glasses. Trickle single cream on top and decorate with fresh berries. Serve warm or cool.

suppliers

The following list includes sources of the ingredients featured in the photographs in this book, as well as other useful suppliers and producers of fine foods.

HERBS, SPICES & CONDIMENTS

The Cool Chile Company
110 Holland Park Avenue,
London W11
Tel: 0870 902 1145
Web: www.coolchile.co.uk
Hard-to-get dried chillies, as well as a range of Mexican foods.

Fox's Spices
Mason's Road, Stratford-upon-Avon, Warwickshire
Tel: 01789 266420
Interesting spices and dried herbs, and good oriental spice mixes.

Peppers by Post
Sea Spring Farm Lyme View,
West Bexington, Dorset
Tel: 01308 897892
Web: www.peppersbypost.biz
Both fresh and dried peppers and chillies, including unusual types.

Sira Cash & Carry
128 The Broadway, Southall,
Middlesex
Tel: 020 8574 2280
Asian grocer with amazing stock.

The Spice Shop
1 Blenheim Crescent,
London W11
Tel: 020 7221 4448. Web:
www.thespiceshoponline.com
Additive-free herbs and spices, and also oddities such as tapioca.

The Wiltshire Tracklement Co.
The Dairy Farm, Pinkney Park,
Sherston, Wiltshire
Tel: 01666 840851
Web: www.tracklements.co.uk
Impressive mustards, chutneys, jellies and other condiments.

CHOCOLATE

The Chocolate Society
36 Elizabeth Street,
London SW1
Tel: 020 7259 9222
Web: www.chocolate.co.uk
Shop sells own-brand and all types of superb Valrhona chocolate.

Richart
258 boulevard St-Germain,
75007 Paris
Tel: +33 1 45 55 66 00
Web: www.richart.fr
Perhaps the best chocolate ever.

Rococo Chocolates
321 Kings Road, London SW3
Tel: 020 7352 5857. Web:
www.rococochocolates.com
Truly remarkable chocolate, in beautiful packaging.

COFFEE, TEA & ALCOHOL

Algerian Coffee Stores
52 Old Compton Street,
London W1
Tel: 020 7437 2480
Web: www.algcoffee.co.uk
Wonderful shop with around 100 different coffees and 140 teas.

Constantine Stores Ltd
30 Fore Street, Constantine,
Falmouth, Cornwall
Tel: 01326 340226
Web: www.drinkfinder.co.uk
Up to 1,700 different spirits, 700 whiskies and 500 wines.

Gerry's Wines and Spirits
74 Old Compton Street,
London W1V
Tel: 020 7734 2053
Staggering range of spirits and wines from all over the world.

Mariage Frères
30 rue Bourg-Tibourg,
75004 Paris
Tel: +33 1 40 51 82 50
Web: www.mariagefreres.com
Venerable tea merchants, with a vast range and bespoke blends.

PRESERVED FRUIT, VEGETABLES, NUTS & SEEDS

A Cracker of a Nut
Tricketts Road, West Melton, RD 6, Christchurch, New Zealand
Tel: +64 3 3478103
Email: crackernut@clear.net.nz
Top-grade walnuts, walnut paste, walnut oil and walnut flour.

Gegenbauer
Naschtmarkt (stand 111–114),
Waldgasse3, A-1100 Vienna
Tel: +43 1 6041 088
Web: www.gegenbauer.at
Great pickled vegetables, as well as oils, vinegars and mustards in Vienna's famous market.

Julian Graves Ltd
Ham Lane, off Stallings Lane,
Kingswinford, West Midlands
Tel: 01384 282700
Dried fruit of excellent quality.

Michanicou Brothers
2 Clarendon Road, London W11
Tel: 020 7727 5191
Famous green grocer's but also has dried mushrooms, fruit and nuts.

Super Bahar
349a Kensington High Street,
London W8
Tel: 020 7603 5083
Treasure trove of dried fruits, nuts and pickles, plus Iranian caviar.

PRESERVED MEATS, SAUSAGES & CHARCUTERIE

Austrian Sausage Centre
10a Belmont Street,
London NW1
Tel: 020 7267 5412
Makers and suppliers of cooked meats, including sausages from Poland, Germany and Austria.

Denhay Farms Ltd
Broadoak, Bridport, Dorset
Tel: 01308 458963/422770
Web: www.denhay.co.uk
Award-winning dry-cured ham and bacon, as well as cheeses.

W A Lidgate Ltd
110 Holland Park Avenue,
London W11
Tel: 020 7727 8243
Superb free-range and organic meats, including charcuterie.

CURED FISH & SEAFOOD

The Achiltibuie Smokehouse (Summer Isles Foods)
Ullapool, Ross-shire IV26
Tel: 01854 622 353
Delicious kippers and oak-smoked eel and haddock. Tasty marinades.

Caviar House
161 Piccadilly, London W1V
Tel: 020 7409 0445
Web: www.caviar-house.com
All kinds of caviar, including rare.

Chalmers and Gray
67 Notting Hill Gate,
London W11
Tel: 020 7221 6177
Superb smoked fish and canned and vac-packed seafood.

H Forman & Son
30a Marshgate Lane,
Stratford, London E15
Tel: 020 8221 3900
Web: www.formanandfield.com
Sensational smoked wild salmon and other smoked seafood.

Loch Fyne Oysters Ltd
Clachan, Cairndow, Argyle PA26
Tel: 01499 600 264
Web: www.lochfyne.com
Famous producers of smoked salmon, haddock, trout and eel, kippers and pickled herring.

Petrossian
18 boulevard de Latour
Maubourg, 75007 Paris
Tel: +33 1 44 11 32 22
Web: www.petrossian.com
Internationally renowned caviar house with extensive range of top-quality caviar and related products.

OILS & VINEGARS

The Albany Olive Oil Company
88 Burne Road, RD 4 Albany,
Auckland, New Zealand
Tel: +64 0 9 4278194. Web:
www.olivesnewzealand.co.nz
Fine selection of extra virgin olive oils, including feral and unfiltered.

Bristol Merchants
20 Fenton Road, Bristol
Tel: 0777 885 1273
Web: www.avocadooil.co.uk
Over 150 oils, including delicious cold-pressed avocado oils from New Zealand.

Maggie Beer
2 Keith Street, Tanunda SA,
Australia
Tel: +61 885630204
Web: www.maggiebeer.com.au
High-quality verjuice, as well as other storecupboard essentials.

The Oil Merchant
47 Ashchurch Grove,
London W12
Tel: 020 8740 1335
Wonderful and inspiring range of oils from all corners of the world, as well as other condiments.

CHEESES & DAIRY PRODUCTS

La Fromagerie
2–4 Moxon St, London W1
(tel: 020 7359 7440), and
30 Highbury Park, London N5
(tel: 020 7935 0341)
Web: www.lafromagerie.co.uk/
Superb cheeses (matured on the premises), as well as other fine foods, including olives and pasta.

I J Mellis Cheesemonger
205 Bruntsfield Place,
Edinburgh EH10
Tel: 0131 447 8889. Web:
www.ijmellischeesemonger.com
Great range of cheeses, as well as teas, coffee and chocolate.

Neal's Yard Dairy
6 Park Street, Borough Market,
London SE1
Tel: 020 7645 3555
Splendid range of cheeses (many artisan varieties), matured on site.

BAKING GOODS

Aberfeldy Water Mill
Mill Street, Aberfeldy PH15
Tel: 01887 820803. Web:
www.aberfeldy-watermill.co.uk
Authentic water mill producing superb pinhead oatmeal.

Billington's Sugar
The Cunard Building,
Liverpool L3 1EL UK
Tel: 0151 243 9001
Web: www.billingtons.co.uk
Producers of a large range of unrefined and organic sugars.

& Clarke's
122 Kensington Church Street,
London W8
Tel: 020 7229 2190
Web: www.sallyclarke.com
Gourmet flours, as well as superb breads, made on site.

Lionel Poilâne
46 Elizabeth Street,
London SW1
Tel: 020 7808 4910
Web: www.poilane.fr
Superb sourdough loaves, and the wheat flour used to make them.

W & H Marriage & Sons Ltd
Chelmer Mills, Chelmsford, Essex
Tel: 01245 354455
Authentic flours and bakery items, including Canadian wheat flour.

The Oatmeal of Alford
Mains of Haulkerton, Laurencekirk, Aberdeenshire AB30
Tel: 019755 62209
Web: www.oatmealofalford.co.uk
Highly regarded organic oatmeal.

Shipton Mill
Long Newnton, Tetbury,
Gloucestershire
Tel: 01666 505050
Stoneground flour for home bakers.

DELICATESSENS, ETHNIC GROCERS & SUPERMARKETS

Archie Foodstore
14 Moscow Rd, London W2
Tel: 020 7229 2275
Small but excellent stock of Greek, Turkish and Middle Eastern foods, including pulses, nuts and syrups.

Brindisa
32 Exmouth Market,
London EC1
Tel: 020 7713 1666
Web: www.brindisa.com
Hard-to-find Spanish foods, including beans, canned fish and meats.

Camisa & Son
61 Old Compton Street,
London W1
Tel: 020 7437 7610
Superb Italian deli selling authentic pasta, oils and dried mushrooms.

Carluccio's
29a Neil Street London WC2
Tel: 020 7240 1487. Web:
www.carluccios.com/plain.html
Impressive range of quality Italian foods, including own-brand pasta.

Mr Christian's
11 Elgin Crescent, London W11
Tel: 020 7229 0501
International deli selling ethnic breads, olives, oils and dry goods.

The Fifth Floor (Food Market)
Harvey Nichols
109–125 Knightsbridge,
London SW1
Tel: 0870 873 3833
Web: www.harveynichols.com
Lush emporium of excellent foods of all kinds – beautifully packaged.

Fresh & Wild
Tel: 020 7229 1063 (head office)
Web: www.freshandwild.co.uk
London-wide chain of organic/ wholefood supermarkets. Good for nuts, dried fruits, grains, seaweed, tofu and Asian condiments.

R García & Sons
248–250 Portobello Road,
London, W11
Tel: 020 7221 6119
Excellent Spanish foods, such as meats, canned fish and dry goods.

A. Gold
42 Brushfield Street, London E1
Tel: 020 7247 2487
Web: www.agold.co.uk
Traditional British foods, from cheeses to confectionery.

The Grocer on Elgin
6 Elgin Crescent, London W11
Tel: 020 7221 3844
Web: www.thegroceron.com
Stylish delicatessen, stockist of Sugar Club products.

Harrods Food Hall
87–135 Brompton Road,
Knightsbridge, London SW1
Tel: 020 7730 1234
Web: www.harrods.com
Splendid charcuterie, cheeses, deli items, dried fruits and nuts.

Jeroboams
96 Holland Park Avenue,
London W11
Tel: 020 7727 9359
Web: www.jeroboams.co.uk
Fine British and European cheeses, olives, oils and wines.

Lupe Pito's Deli
24 Leven Street, Edinburgh EH3
Tel: 0131 228 6241
Web: www.lupepintos.com
Caribbean, Central American and Spanish foods. Also in Glasgow.

Oriental City
399 Edgware Road,
London NW9
Tel: 020 8200 0009
Web: www.oriental-city.com
Huge choice of Japanese, Chinese and Southeast Asian foods.

Panzers
13–19 Circus Road, St Johns
Wood, London NW8
Tel: 020 7722 8596
Superb Jewish deli items, dry goods and some American groceries.

Pat's Chung Ying Chinese Supermarket
199 Leith Walk, Edinburgh EH6
Tel: 0131 554 0358. Web: www.-yell.co.uk/sites/patschungying/
Wide selection of oriental produce.

Selfridges Food Hall
400 Oxford Street, London W1
Tel: 08708 377 377
Web: www.selfridges.co.uk
Excellent range of dry goods, preserves, pickles and deli items.

Speck
2 Holland Park Terrace,
Portland Road, London W11
Tel: 020 7229 7005
Excellent Italian deli products, condiments and salamis.

Stein's Seafood Delicatessen
Riverside, Padstow,
Cornwall PL28
Tel: 01841 532700
High-quality specialist ingredients, including canned tuna, anchovies and sardines.

Talad Thai
320 Upper Richmond Road,
London SW15
Tel: 020 8789 8084
Thai and Asian groceries.

Tawana Oriental Supermarket
18–20, Chepstow Road,
London, W2
Tel: 020 7221 6316
Lively stores selling vast range of Vietnamese, Thai, Korean and Filipino food.

Valvona & Crolla
19 Elm Row, Edinburgh EH7
Tel: 0131 556 6066
Web: www.valvonacrolla.com
Famous, exuberant and authentic Italian deli with huge range of high-quality produce.

Villandry
170 Great Portland Street,
London W1
Tel: 020 7631 3131
High-class deli foods, cheeses, wines and dry goods.

Wing Yip
395 Edgeware Road,
London NW2
Tel: 020 8450 0422
Diverse selection of Far Eastern, mainly Chinese products.

Waitrose (supermarket)
Tel: 020 7370 2424 (head office)
Web: www.waitrose.com
Excellent range of everyday, ethnic and select food items including dried mushrooms, fruits in syrup, pickled vegetables, and charcuterie.

bibliography

Alexander, Stephanie, *The Cook's Companion* (Viking, 1996).

Bayless, Rick and Deann Groen, *Authentic Mexican – Regional Cooking from the Heart of Mexico* (William Morrow & Company, 1987)

Beer, Maggie. *Maggie's Table* (Viking, 2001)

Bharadwaj, Monisha, *The Indian Pantry* (Kyle Cathie, 1996)

Blanc, Raymond, *Foolproof French Cookery* (BBC Books, 2002)

Garten, Ina, *Barefoot Contessa Parties!* (Clarkson Potter Publisher, 2001)

Gayler, Paul, *Flavours of the World* (Kyle Cathie, 2002)

Owen, Sri, *Noodles the New Way* (Quadrille, 2000)

Puck, Wolfgang, *Pizza, Pasta and More* (Random House, 2000)

Roden, Claudia, *The Book of Jewish Food* (Knopf, 1997)

Roux, Michel, *Sauces* (Quadrille, 1996)

Salaman, Rena, *Greek Food* (Harper Collins, 1993)

Stein, Rick, *Rick Stein's Food Heroes* (BBC Books, 2002)

Vongerichten, Jean-Georges, and Mark Bittman, *Cooking at Home with a Four-Star Chef* (Broadway Books, 1998)

Wolfert, Paula, *The Cooking of South West France* (Grub Street, 1999)

acknowledgements

AUTHOR: This book has been a huge undertaking, and teamwork was essential. My heartfelt thanks to the following friends, colleagues, researchers and assistants, without whom this book would still be languishing in the drawer: Vicki Peterson, for research, tasting and word processing; Janine Ratcliffe, Bob Larkins and Barrabel Mason for research, testing and tasting; Pippa Cuthbert for research, testing, tasting and word processing; Emma Robertson for testing and tasting; also Janine Ratcliffe and Emma McIntosh for food styling assistance. Many thanks also to Emily Hatchwell, Janet James, Madeline Weston, David Munns and Victoria Allen for their support above and beyond the call of duty.

PUBLISHER: We would like to thank the following for contributing recipes to this book (in order of appearance): Rick and Deann Groen Bayless, Jean-Georges Vongerichten, Rena Salaman, Maggie Beer, Raymond Blanc, Michel Roux, Claudia Roden, Paul Gayler, Rick Stein, Paula Wolfert, Wolfgang Puck, Stephanie Alexander, Monisha Bharadwaj, Ina Garten and Sri Owen.

All guest recipes are used with permission.

index